AUTHORS-AT-ARMS

RICHARD STEELE

Private Gentleman (Cadet), Life Guards;
Ensign and Captain, Coldstream Guards;
Captain, 34th (Lord Lucas's) Foot (now
1st Batt. The Border Regiment)

EDWARD GIBBON

Captain, Major, and Lieutenant-Colonel,
South Hants Battalion, The Hampshire
Regiment of Militia (now the 3rd Batt.
The Hampshire Regiment)

SAMUEL TAYLOR COLERIDGE

Private, 15th (Eliott's) Light Dragoons
(now the 15th King's Royal Hussars)

WALTER SCOTT

Quartermaster, Royal Edinburgh Light
Dragoons, Midlothian Yeomanry Cavalry

WALTER SAVAGE LANDOR

Coronel de la Infantería del Ejército
Real de España

LORD BYRON

Brigade-Commander (Archistrategos),
Greek Army of Independence,
1824

THE PRIVATE GENTLEMAN CADET

AUTHORS-AT-ARMS

The Soldiering of
SIX GREAT WRITERS

by CHARLES PASCOE HAWKES

WITH SEVEN ILLUSTRATIONS BY THE AUTHOR

Essay Index Reprint Series

originally published by
MACMILLAN & CO., LIMITED

BOOKS FOR LIBRARIES PRESS
FREEPORT, NEW YORK

First Published 1934
Reprinted 1970

STANDARD BOOK NUMBER:
8369-1511-9

LIBRARY OF CONGRESS CATALOG CARD NUMBER:
70-107709

PRINTED IN THE UNITED STATES OF AMERICA

Icil chevalchent en guise de baruns dreites lur hanstes, fermez lur gunfanuns.

(These ride with the high air of fighting men, their spears erect
and battle-pennons furled.)

CHANSON DE ROLAND

*   *   *

Sword and Pen are at best alternative weapons, jealously incompatible; the same hand seldom succeeds with both.

CALDERON

*   *   *

To rescue from the past the fading figures of great men;
To select from the annals such facts as shall give truth to portraiture;
To set dead heroes in the light of day——

CHARLES WHIBLEY

PREAMBLE

OF the six authors whose military history is here set forth, Steele soldiered for advancement in arms or literature—whichever should turn up trumps; Gibbon and Scott from patriotism, and, in the latter's case, horse-exercise; Landor and Byron from their love of Liberty; and Coleridge in despair. Two of the six were cavalrymen unequivocally; one left the Household Cavalry for the Foot Guards; two were of the Infantry by choice, and one served only as a Brigadier. Five were both poets and prose-writers, and one an historian. Landor and Byron alone saw active service.

ACKNOWLEDGMENTS

THE Author's thanks are due to Colonel the Earl of Selborne, Lieutenant-Colonel Sir Morgan Crofton, Bart., and Captain the Earl of Stratheden and Campbell, for assistance and information relating to their respective regiments; and to the Editors and Proprietors of *The Nineteenth Century and After* and *The Cornhill Magazine* for permission to reprint such of the chapters as have already appeared in those periodicals. He must ask all those others by whose previous work he has profited herein to regard the 'List of Authorities' at the end of the book as a very grateful acknowledgment of numerous obligations.

CONTENTS

CONTENTS

LIST OF ILLUSTRATIONS

RICHARD STEELE

Private Gentleman (Cadet)—LIFE GUARDS
Ensign and *Captain*—COLDSTREAM GUARDS
Captain—34TH (LORD LUCAS'S) FOOT (now the
1ST BATT. THE BORDER REGIMENT)

I

A PRIVATE GENTLEMAN OF THE LIFE GUARDS

> When he mounted a war-horse with a great sword in his hand
> and planted himself behind King William III against Louis
> XIV, he lost the succession to a very good estate in the county
> of Wexford, from the same humour which he has pursued ever
> since; of preferring the state of his mind to that of his
> fortune. When he cocked his hat and put on a broadsword,
> jackboots, and a shoulder-belt under the command of the
> unfortunate Duke of Ormonde, he was not acquainted with
> his own parts.   *Theatre*, No. 11

'*Arma virumque—*'

Dick Steele of Merton, a sound Latinist enough since
the days when Bartlett's ferule had beaten Virgil's hexa-
meters into him at Charterhouse, made up his mind that,
for a man in his position—a penniless Irishman with no
definite prospects on leaving Oxford—the Army was undoubtedly the thing. He had been born, like Swift, his
senior by five years, in the parish of St. Bride's, Dublin.
His father, an attorney of the King's Inns, had died when
he was five, and his mother soon afterwards. He owed his
education at school and the University to his guardian,
Henry Gascoigne, his mother's brother and then confidential secretary to His Grace of Ormonde, his influence
with whom three years before had obtained for the boy,

3

already a Charterhouse Exhibitioner at Christ Church, a
'Postmastership' at Merton. Dick (he was the sort of
Richard whom most men, and all women, *must* call 'Dick')
had enjoyed himself hugely at Oxford on a minimum of
work and a maximum of high spirits and extravagance. In
the company of Joe Addison—his closest crony at Charterhouse and later a *Demy* at Magdalen, a shy fastidious
scholar with an enviable knack of prose—he had read a
little and roistered much; swapped squibs with Christopher
Codrington of All Souls over claret and oysters at the
Oxford coffee-house (the prototype of all those over which
in London afterwards he was to reign supreme); phil-
andered by moonlight at the back gate of Merton garden—
hortus blandulus optimus recessus—with young ladies of the
city; and written comedies which he had burnt when told
by candid friends that they were rubbish. In 1689, at
seventeen, he had come up from Charterhouse; and now, in
1694, at two-and-twenty, he was still *in statu pupillari*.
Joe Addison had taken his degree, and at the Magdalen
High Table was the coming man whose Latin poems were
praised by even the great John Dryden; and Kit Codrington, now an Ensign in the Coldstream Guards, was dis-
tinguishing himself at the front in Flanders. Dick felt
uncommonly lonely, and missed most of all his daily
companionship with Addison. In their psychology the pair
were complementary; the one reticent and sensitive, the
other, ebullient with a lively and sympathetic interest in
the world around him, drawing out the best and most
human qualities of his friend. But Dick, whose prospects

were at best precarious, was prone to action rather than refinements of thought; while Joe, secure in the background of a happy home and his own attainments, had scope for quiet intellectual endeavour. Money matters were pressing, too, with Dick—as they always had been and ever were to be. He must earn or starve. Uncle Henry's purse was not bottomless, nor the Ormonde interest indefinitely flexible. Although in his rare moments of introspection he was religiously inclined, he felt no urge to the Church and a College living; he was tired enough of Oxford not to desiderate Dondom; and from the Law he recoiled in contemptuous horror. Kit Codrington was right; a poet, a wit, an orator and essayist, he had chosen the sword; like an Elizabethan, he had not considered Arms and the Toga incompatible. Adventure and advancement offered themselves abundantly in the King's service; no man could write convincingly in any form without a groundwork of experience, and in those days there was no such fertile field of experience as there was in Arms. (How Dick, on reading Tom Tickell's *Oxford* thirteen years afterwards, must have been gratified by a sense of decision rightly taken!—

> When Codrington and Steele their verse unrein,
> And form an easy, unaffected strain,
> A double wreath of laurel binds their brow,
> For both are Poets and both are Warriors too.)

He dared not, however, ask the Duke, through Gascoigne, for an actual commission; but His Grace, a hero of Steinkirk and Landen and a favourite of King William,

5

happened also to be Colonel-Captain of the 2nd or Queen's Troop of the Life Guards (in which regiment, conveniently enough, Dr. Welbore Ellis, Dick's "Lov'd Tutour" at Christ Church, was now a chaplain). Surely, as Colonel in the Household Cavalry, the Duke might be induced to concede a cadetship, though as Chancellor of the University a postmastership had been the sole product of his patronage, to Gascoigne's nephew. Moreover, Dick had all the Dublin Irishman's love of horseflesh, and, if he was to soldier, he gallantly if lazily preferred the mounted arm. His mind made up, he determined to lose no time. He put himself 'out of commons' at the Merton buttery, promised to pay a score of his more pressing bills, and left Oxford degreeless but undaunted on January the 12th, taking with him "the love of the whole society of Merton College". An interview with his uncle at the Duke's house in St. James's Square, and a later and more formidable one with the Duke himself, were followed by visits to the tailors and the Army Office in Whitehall; and within a few weeks the postmaster of Merton became a 'Private Gentleman (Cadet)' in His Majesty's Life Guards.

* * * * *

In January 1661 King Charles II had raised three troops of Life Guards, designated respectively the 1st or King's Troop, the 2nd or the Duke of York's Troop, and the 3rd or the Duke of Albemarle's Troop; together with a 'Royal Regiment of Horse' of eight troops, under Aubrey de Vere, Earl of Oxford. The former subsequently

became the 1st and 2nd Life Guards, and the latter the
Royal Horse Guards (Blues). The Life Guards were from
the beginning the Sovereign's personal bodyguard and part
of his Household, with peculiar and original privileges as
such; but the 'Royal Regiment of Horse', though closely
attached to His Majesty's person, did not actually or
officially become Household Cavalry in the same sense
until a century and a half later. (It is noteworthy, with
reference to its original C.O., that down to Victorian times
this corps was often and commonly referred to as 'the
Oxford Blues'.) During the whole of Charles's reign these
regiments, together with the Foot Guards and the re-
patriated garrisons of Dunkirk and Tangier, constituted
the nucleus of the standing Army which, in the teeth of
Parliamentary opposition, he was determined to maintain.
King James II and William III added other units as their
policy dictated.

The distrust of a standing Army which had originated
during the Protectorate had continued under Charles and
James: but under William the Jacobite danger and the
aggressive ambition of Louis XIV demanded military
action on the Continent and therefore the existence of
Regular Forces. The Army, however, had as yet no legal
existence. There were no constitutional sanctions for the
enforcement of military discipline, and the Cromwellian
powers of billeting in private premises had been abolished.
By the Mutiny Act, however, Parliament conferred on the
King's Officers the powers requisite for the maintenance
of discipline, and provision was also made for the proper

pay of the Forces; but both these powers were only granted from year to year, as, indeed, they still are; for the Mutiny Act, like the granting of Civil Supply, has remained annual ever since the Revolution. As to quarters, no barracks were as yet in existence: though at intervals Somerset House and Whitehall, and even Windsor, when not occupied by the Royal Family, were used as quarters for the Life Guards and the Foot Guards. The Savoy and the Tower of London were also used for this purpose, but otherwise the Companies of the Foot Guards were quartered in billets about London, arranged for by the Company Commanders individually with the authorities of the various parishes. On his accession in 1688 William removed the British Guards from duty at the Royal Palaces, in favour of his Dutch Guard Regiments. But in 1689 Parliament insisted on the withdrawal of these and the restoration to the British Household Troops of their duty-privileges at the Royal Residences.

In 1690 the 2nd Troop of the Life Guards had been recalled from Marlborough's Forces in Flanders for duty, under the new name of 'The Queen's Troop', as personal bodyguard to Queen Mary. In 1694, when Steele took his place in its ranks as a 'Private Gentleman (Cadet)', the Troop was commanded by James 2nd Duke of Ormonde as Colonel-Captain, and consisted of 16 Officers, 5 N.C.O.'s, and 200 'Private Gentlemen'. By Royal Warrant every grade of Officer in the Life Guards was entitled to rank far above his nominal position; by reason, probably, of the high military rank already held by those who received the earliest commissions—of the four original Lieutenants, for instance, one was a Major-General and another a full Colonel. The Captain of the Troop ranked as a Colonel, the senior Subalterns as Lieutenant-Colonels, and the juniors as Majors; and many ex-Captains were among the troopers, who were officially addressed on parade as 'Gentlemen of the Life Guards'. (Down to quite modern times the prefix "Mr." appeared before every Lifeguards-man's name on the muster-roll.) The Regiment was supreme in precedence, and the pay of the 'Private Gentle-men' was generous; while the Cadets were young men of position and education but small means whose families had neither the influence to procure nor the money to buy a commission for them, and who were content to serve in this probationary grade until a turn of fortune should lead to a commission or some office of profit outside the Army. The Life Guards were armed with carbines, straight heavy swords, and long horse-pistols; and though on service all ranks wore stout buff-coats, their peace-time uniform was magnificent, as befitted the English equivalent of Louis XIV's *Maison de Roy*. The 'Private Gentlemen' and Cadets of the 2nd or Queen's Troop wore broad-brimmed hats with lace and loops of gold, breast and back-plates of steel, carbine-belts of green velvet (green being the troop colour), cloaks and coats of scarlet lined with blue and laced with gold and silver, high-flapped dragoon boots and long-necked spurs. Their horse-furniture and holster-covers were of scarlet and gold; the ribbons on their horses' bridles, manes, and cruppers were of green taffeta, and they carried a standard and guidon of green damask with the royal crown and cipher. The kettle-drummers and trumpeters were gorgeous in gold jackets, as they are to-day; and the troop section of horse-grenadiers (whose duties in the field assimilated to those of mounted infantry and bombers combined) had jackets with green loops and yellow tufts, and were accompanied on parade not by a trumpeter, but, by some curious and unexplained tradition, a hautboy player: also, they carried arquebuses instead of carbines and bayonets instead of swords. Such was the distinguished corps into whose ranks Dick Steele was admitted as a Cadet on the authority of its Commanding Officer, whose grandfather, as a Governor of the School, had signed his nomination paper for Charterhouse eleven years before.

Years afterwards Steele wrote in the *Tatler* (No. 164) of his experiences as "a cadet in the King's Army" on parade with his troop at Whitehall or Kensington or Hampton Court, "mounted on black horses" (as to-day) "with white feathers in our hats and scarlet coats richly laced": while the *London Post*, a contemporary journal, described His Majesty's Life Guards as "extraordinary grand and thought to be the finest body of Horse in the world". The Gentlemen of the Life Guards, indeed, were no rough common troopers, no such "Hulking Toms", as Thackeray describes in *Esmond*; nor was "poor Dick Steele" a "singular trooper", conscripted by force of his own circumstances, a 'gentleman-ranker' who found that his Charterhouse and Oxford education made him exceptional among his com-

rades. In the main, Thackeray's picture of Steele in
Esmond is as sympathetically untrue as Macaulay's bitter
attack on him in the *Essay on Addison* is unsympathetically
misleading. 'Mr. Steele, Cadet in the Life Guards', was, in
fact, proud of his uniform and position. He began to hold
his own with the wits and men-of-fashion in the coffee-
houses, and to frequent a polite and cultivated society. He
had an unquenchable zest for life and the acutest faculty
of observation and discernment, with an itch to write
about it all in prose or verse. He could turn a good verse,
sportive or serious, with the best of them; and in the
graceful fashion of the day could scribble a complimentary
couplet to any pretty woman while she waited.

Such a scrawl still survives in the Marlborough MSS.,
and its lines relate to a Mrs. Selwyn (the wife—or daughter
—of a Brigadier who had served with the King and the
Duke of Ormonde in Holland), whom at some party he
had drawn by lot as his 'Valentine'.

> One minute, Fortune, thou has let me live,
> I truly all my life before forgive,
> Cares did till now my rising bliss destroy,
> And streaks of sorrow ran through all my joy.
> But, fickle Goddess, thou art now sincere,
> Quite happy now, I feel not hope nor fear;
> Thy wealth and Empire on thy slaves bestow,
> Slaves who no bliss but wealth and Empire know.
> Be all thy power in one great gift display'd,
> And to these arms convey the lovely maid,
> I never will beseech thy bounty more,
> Be thou as rough and angry as before.

An Irishman's blarney, no doubt; but in a ballad inspired by the boudoir rather than the barrack-room, composed for a lady of elegance, and scarcely congruous with Thackeray's caricature of the drunken detrimental ranker. It is true that Dick lamented the unmilitary frivolity of his muse:

> Instead of troops in battle mix'd
> And Gauls on British spears transfix'd,
> She paints the soft distress and mien
> Of dames expiring of the spleen.

But Thackeray failed to ascertain the actual status of a 'Private Gentleman (Cadet)' in the Life Guards, and so misdrew his vignette of Steele in *Esmond*. It was about this time, too, that Dick first met 'Rivella', Mrs. de la Rivière Manley, a young lady of good looks and some literary talent who found him then undoubtedly attractive, but who, having fallen later upon evil days, became a paid political lampooner and savagely attacked him. The daughter of Sir Robert Manley, Governor of Londonderry Fort at the time of the Revolution, she had as a young girl been tricked into a bogus marriage with John Manley, her scapegrace cousin, who on the discovery of his fraud had deserted her. Broken and embittered, she had come to London and attached herself to the Duchess of Cleveland, in whose dissolute circle she developed a cynical unscrupulousness. That she was an intimate, and afterwards an enemy, of Dick Steele's is clear; for fourteen years later she libelled him in false yet familiar detail in her *New Atlantis*, after having been convicted meanwhile of forgery of a public document. But Rivella's admiration of Dick was more constant than she thought, and in 1717 she dedicated a play to him, expressing the deepest contrition for her previous obloquies.

Though he had leisure to enjoy society, training for his chosen profession occupied much more of Steele's time. The failure of the previous year's campaign in the Low Countries had led to its renewal by King William, and Codrington, now a Captain, was with his Coldstreamers before Namur: Ireland was still dangerously sulky after the Boyne, and the Scottish Highlanders sullen after Glencoe. The prospect of active service drew Dick on; for unless he could win favour somehow with an influential military or political personage in London—or borrow the money to pay for it—his hope of a commission lay in War. But, as Steele's enemies were afterwards to sneer, with him the pen was mightier than the sword. A poem was to gain him promotion from the ranks; he was to owe his Ensigncy to an Elegy.

*   *   *   *   *

Queen Mary II died of smallpox in the last week of December 1694. Her body was embalmed; and three months later her funeral procession wound its way in State from Whitehall to Henry VII's Chapel in the Abbey, outside which the 2nd Troop of the Life Guards, the dead Queen's own troop, was drawn up. And as the emotional Dick—his uniform and accoutrements swathed in sombre marks of mourning—sat on his black charger and watched the long cortège winding its way to Westminster in a silence broken only by the minute guns and the passing bell, his feelings and impressions grouped themselves quite naturally in his head into a verse-epitome of the nation's grief, which he determined to commit to paper before the day was over. Behind the leading troops with their muffled drums walked the great Statesmen and Lords of Parliament, followed by the Commons—the latter's variance with the King veiled for that day beneath their mourning garments. Then came the dead Queen's Special Master-of-the-Horse (Mary had had all the Stuart's discerning love of horseflesh) leading her favourite charger, which seemed to the impressionable Dick "to heave big sighs when it would neigh". Next came the funeral car with its pathetic pomp of nodding plumes, followed by the Queen's ladies, among them Lady Derby, the Colonel's sister; and finally more troops, marching with arms reversed. The King was absent, prostrate with grief—or, as some Jacobite cynics said, remorse. But Dick was fairer:

> Since his kind frame can't the large suffering bear
> In pity to his people he's not here:
> For to the mighty loss we now receive,
> The next affliction were to see him grieve.

And so the Stuart half of the Dual Monarchy was extinguished. And while her father at St. Germain's, financed by the French King, was busy preparing another armed force to carry war into her country, Anne Hyde's daughter, a reigning Queen of England, still young—she was only two-and-thirty—and beloved by all her subjects, was carried graveward past the window where within the memory of men then living the head of her sainted grand-

father had been displayed above the block for the execration
of his people.

* * * * *

Dick Steele rode back to quarters with the half-formed
verses ringing in his head; genuine emotion and a sense of
peculiar opportunity appropriate to his gifts incongruously
combining in his brain. No time was to be lost; poets and
poetasters would clutch at such a theme, and in a day or
two the town would be glutted with elegies.

His pen flew feverishly across the paper, and within a
few hours the thing was finished. He was determined that
it should be published anonymously, so as at once to
stimulate curiosity and interest and to cover up possible
failure. Then came the question (of paramount importance
to an Augustan author) to whom to dedicate it with the best
hope of resulting benefit? To the King? Such dedications
would be two-a-penny: and William, while, as the alien
residue of the Dual Monarchy he might be gratified by
such proofs of loyalty, might also half resent them as
intrusive on his personal grief. To the Duke, his Colonel-
Captain? That would be, even for Dick, a little too pointed,
and would be following too closely the granting of the
cadetship. To the brilliant Jack Churchill, Earl of Marlborough? But he was now suspect with the King and had
been in the Tower less than two years since. Then, at his
wits' end, Steele had an inspiration. Why not dedicate it
to John Cutts?—Lord Cutts of Gowran, Governor of the
Isle of Wight, a poet, an Irishman, a notable soldier, and,
most important of all, a Colonel in the same Regiment of

Foot Guards as Kit Codrington. Even Swift admitted that Cutts was a fighting soldier, "a Salamander in action", and the Dean's sneers at his "lack of intelligence" are difficult to reconcile with the admittedly sound though unheeded advice given by Cutts at the disastrous landing operations in Camaret Bay during the previous year. He was a personal favourite of both William and the Queen, to whom he had inscribed a volume of *Poetical Exercises* in 1687. Dick had a fleeting day-dream in which he saw himself, an Ensign at last, carrying the King's Colour in the Coldstream. Hot-foot, then, to Bennet the publisher's in St. Paul's Churchyard: and in no time at all a folio pamphlet with a black-bordered title-page (an advance copy of which had early been dispatched to Carisbrooke, Lord Cutts's official residence as Governor of The Wight) was on sale at all the London booksellers:

"THE PROCESSION
a
POEM
on
Her Majesty's
FUNERAL
By a Gentleman of The Army
Motto: 'Fungar inani Munere'—Virgil

[How that would have pleased old Bartlett at Charterhouse!]

London, Printed for Thomas Bennet at the Half Moon in St. Paul's Churchyard, 1695.

To the Right Honourable The Lord Cutts——"

Then, under date of March 19, 1695, followed forty-two
lines of the ornatest dedication, extolling the late Queen's
virtues and the exploits, valour, and character of the
dedicatee—"whom Death has so often allured with the
glory of dangers and the beauty of wounds"; and con-
cluding by a declaration of "the fervent ambition I have
long had of expressing myself, My Lord, Your Lordship's
most passionate admirer and most devoted humble servant". The poem itself, in which the influence of most of
his contemporary poets is discernible, describes the solemn
occasion in rhetorical detail, with such imagery as the
grandiose style of the period demanded and many moral
reflections on mortality and man's suffering lot. Though
cruder than his maturer verse, it is charged with live
emotion and genuine patriotic feeling.

Steele's titled and influential trout rose with amazing
alacrity to this funereal fly. Lord Cutts sent for the poet-
Cadet, took an impetuous fancy to him at sight, and at
once set about to obtain for him an Ensigncy in his regiment. Such an instantaneous success was indeed a tribute
to Steele's attractive personality; for it can have been no
mere affair of looks. Dick was a sturdy, thickset, genial
figure, in whose plump face the dark vivacious eyes set
beneath thick black eyebrows were the sole indications of
any unusual intelligence. And Cutts, then thirty-four, was
no vapid courtier to be flattered into friendship, but a man
of wide experience and ripe judgment who knew men and
cities and had travelled and fought in foreign countries.
The two, however, had much in common: both were

Irishmen educated at one of the older universities—Cutts's family came from Gowran in Tyrone though they lived in Essex, and after having been a Fellow-Commoner at St. Catherine's, Cambridge, he was now an LL.D. of that University. Both were poets; the Colonel had published a long poem *La Muse de Cavalier*, as well as his *Poetical Exercises*; and Loth had soldiering ambitions, which in Cutts's case were still ungratified, though he had served as Adjutant-General on the staff of the Duke of Lorraine against the Turks at Buda, and had won his peerage with the Guards under William at the Boyne. At that very time he was under orders to join the Staff at Namur, where he was to distinguish himself by conspicuous gallantry during the siege. Pending the signature of the commission he took Steele into his private service as confidential secretary, leaving him in charge of his finances and his papers and correspondence. And so, within a week or two, Dick had dismounted for the last time from his black troop-horse; and, comfortably settled in Lord Cutts's house in Kensington, began to devote himself to his secretarial duties while awaiting, with such patience as he could command, the arrival of his commission. Such was the power of the pen with cultured patrons in an Augustan age.

CAPTAIN IN THE COLDSTREAM

II

IN THE COLDSTREAM

I remember him almost t'other day but a wretched common trooper: he had the luck to write a small poem, and dedicates it to a person whom he never saw; a Lord, who had a sparkling genius, lov'd the Muses, and was a very good soldier. He encouraged his performance, took him into his family, and gave him a Standard in his regiment. The genteel company that he was let into, assisted by his own genius, wiped off the rust of education. He began to polish his manners, to refine his conversation, and, in short, to fit himself for something better than what he had been used.

RIVELLA MANLEY: *The New Atlantis,* 1709

Soon after Dick joined the Foot Guards in the early autumn of 1695, the King reviewed his Household Regiments, all ranks in which had been fitted with new uniforms for the occasion; and it is reasonable to suppose that Dick's day-dream at last came true and that Ensign Steele, as junior subaltern, carried a Coldstream Colour past his Sovereign. The Regiment of Coldstream Guards was formed at Coldstream in Berwickshire in 1650, from five companies each of Hesilrige's and Fenwick's regiments of Foot; and was thereafter known as Monk's, and later the Lord General's, Foot. In 1661 with all similar units it was disbanded, and laid down its arms on parade on Tower Hill—only to take them up again immediately as

19

'The Lord General's Regiment of Guards'. On Monk's death nine years later it became officially the Coldstream Guards. Of its sister-regiments in the Brigade, the Grenadiers were formed by Charles II in Flanders before the Restoration as 'The Royal Regiment of Guards', a skeleton formation of Officers for his bodyguard when he should 'come into his own again': and after this had happened in 1661 the regiment was reformed as 'The Royal Regiment', later The 1st Regiment of His Majesty's Guards. The Scots Guards had been raised in Edinburgh at the Restoration and remained in Scotland until 1686, when one of their two battalions came south to London, and was for the first time brigaded with the Grenadiers and the Coldstream on the Household establishment. The Coldstream, from its association with the King and Monk, his impresario of the Restoration, had been from the first a *corps d'élite*. Its Officers, like those of the other two Household regiments, were attached to the Court and had the *entrée* at all the great houses. In 1695 it consisted of 44 Officers, 194 N.C.O.'s, and 780 rank-and-file, organized in twelve companies; the first three of which were commanded by the Colonel commanding the Regiment, the Lieutenant-Colonel, and the Major; the senior subaltern being styled the 'Captain-Lieutenant' and being in command of the Colonel's company when the latter was engaged on Regimental duties. The arms were swords and muskets: the Captains carried pikes, the Lieutenants partizans (a kind of halberd), and the Ensigns half-pikes, except when bearing the Colours. The uniform was a long-skirted scarlet coat with blue facings, blue breeches, and white stockings; and the details of cut and lacing varied from time to time with the changes of civilian fashion. The hats were wide-brimmed and black, and the Officers wore curling white feathers. As to-day, the Brigade of Guards, of which the Coldstream was the second senior unit, was the pattern of the Army; and though essentially the Sovereign's bodyguard of Foot, the most efficient and reliable portion of his fighting troops. Such was the corps in whose commissioned ranks by the astute employment of his literary talents a place had been won by the penniless son of an obscure Dublin attorney. Whether it was the example of his Oxford friend Kit Codrington of All Souls that exercised a subconscious bias towards the Coldstream in the trend of Steele's military ambitions, or that the thing came about by reason of a brain-wave in the dedication of *The Funeral* to their Colonel, remains an enigma. But it is indisputable that if at the expiry of his cadetship in the Life Guards he had failed to attain in some way to a position which secured him a place in the *beau monde* of brains and breeding, he would probably have sunk to the squalid level of a Grub Street hack.

Dick's pay as a Coldstreamer Ensign was £106, 9s. 2d. a year, equivalent in modern currency to about £300; and it is remarkable that his first four years' service in commissioned rank is the only period of his life when there is no record of any proceedings for debt against him. He was attached to the Headquarters Company; but, as a sort of unofficial A.D.C. and secretary to the Colonel, spent most

of his time at Carisbrooke—where Cutts was still Governor
of The Wight—and in the mansion at Kensington, where
he was treated by his Commanding Officer "almost as a
son or brother". His chief companion among the Coldstream Officers was Jacob Abady, the regimental surgeon,
a friend of his Uncle Gascoigne at Ormonde House—
through whom Dick still maintained contact with the
Ducal influence. Abady, a smart Officer and a man of
the fashionable world, acted in many matters as Cutts's
steward, and, as a fine horseman and something of a 'vet',
looked after the Colonel's stud, the expenses of which Dick
Steele defrayed from Cutts's privy purse. (Abady, like
Gascoigne, was given in later life a sinecure as 'Tailcart-
taker-in' on the Board of Green Cloth.) Dick was indeed
in clover throughout these years, though his hopes of active
service remained unfulfilled and his literary ambitions
were temporarily in abeyance. He frequented the coffee-
houses—White's, and Wills's, and 'The Grecian'—with
Dryden and Codrington, Sedley, Vanbrugh, and Garth;
lounged in the Mall and ruffled it at routs; though he must
have been sufficiently assiduous in his military duties, for
in 1700 he was gazetted Captain—the highest military
rank to which he was destined to attain, and which, even
after his retirement, he continued to use until it was
eclipsed in 1715 by the sublimer glory of a knighthood.
And now came a momentary return to poesy, evoked, not
by a neglected muse, but by his affection for his dearest
friend. For some reason or other Sir Richard Blackmore,
the King's physician-in-ordinary, had incurred the enmity

of the Wits, who considered him dull and oppressively virtuous. He was an amateur theologian and poet who had written a *Paraphrase on the Book of Job* and an Arthurian epic in twenty-two volumes. Dryden, just before his death in 1700, attacked the *Paraphrase*: and Blackmore retaliated by a *Satire against Wit*. Whereupon, Codrington, Sedley, Lord Anglesey, Steele and others, countered with a pamphlet of anti-Blackmore epigrams, Steele's share in which was a set of verses protesting against a mock-sympathetic allusion to his friend in the *Satire*, which ran *"Heav'ns guard poor Addison!"* They began with an ironical dedication —"To the Mirror of British Knighthood, the worthy author of the *Satire against Wit*; occasioned by the Hemistich on p. 8, Heav'ns guard poor A——n!": and went on,

> Must I, then, passive stand, and can I hear
> The Man I love abused, and yet forbear?
> Impenetrably dull, secure thou'rt found,
> And can'st receive no more than give a wound;

and continued in this strain for twenty lines or so. Sir Richard retorted with some *Discommendatory Verses* which included some, in an unexpectedly jovial vein, directed "To the Noble Captain who was in a d——d confounded pet because the author was pleased to pray for his friend!"

* * * * *

Steele's reputation as a man-of-fashion in the first year of the eighteenth century would have suffered if he had not had at least one duel to his credit. In his *Apology* of the following year he states that "one or two of his acquaintances thought fit to misuse him and try their valour upon him"—with what result it is not recorded. But in 1700 he fought a young Irish Officer, Captain Kelly, in Hyde Park; and the incident was duly reported in the current Press. Apparently, Kelly told Dick that he intended to challenge another man who had, as he thought, affronted him. And Dick's dissuasion of him from that purpose was misinterpreted by Kelly's companions to him as being due, not to disinterested motives, but to Dick's close friendship with the affronter.

Kelly, in consequence, at once proceeded to challenge Dick himself, who, with some compunction, accepted the *cartel*. On the night of Sunday, June 18, the two Irish Officers and their seconds met by moonlight in Hyde Park. When all was ready, the buckle of Dick's right shoe broke, and he used the interval to try and persuade his opponent to an honourable reconciliation; for though no fire-eater, he was conscious of being the better swordsman of the two. The other Irishman, however, was truculent, and the duel proceeded. Kelly attacked with fury, and for some time Dick contented himself with passes while he waited for an opening to disarm or, at most, disable his antagonist. But Kelly pressed so fiercely that there was nothing for it but to run him through the body. For some time his life was despaired of, and official notice had to be taken of the affair. Lord Cutts, however, on an investigation of the facts warmly defended his own Officer, and on Kelly's recovery the principals were reconciled. In the *Theatre* (No. 26) and the *Tatler* (No. 25) Steele registered

his condemnation of duelling; and two years after the
Kelly fight, in his comedy *The Lying Lover* he made a constable say to an Officer—"There's a man killed in the
garden: you're a fine gentleman, so it must be you who
killed him, for good honest people only *beat* one another".
His views were thus much in advance of his time; for,
whether by natural skill or as a result of his Army training,
he was undoubtedly an accomplished master-of-fence. In
1701 Dick was on Detachment at the Tower, where he
continued a life 'about Town' in which wine and women
played parts conformable with the fashionable standard of
the time. He got to know Jacob Tonson, the big book-
seller of the day who was afterwards to be his publisher;
and an intrigue with Tonson's pretty daughter, a minx
of almost twentieth-century audacity, resulted in the expense to him of an illegitimate child. Neither father nor
daughter appear to have resented the occurrence seriously,
and it certainly had no effect, socially or in business, on
the former's subsequent relations with Captain Steele. (*A
propos* the child, soon after his second marriage in 1707
Steele asked his new wife to go with him on a visit which
he proposed to make that afternoon. In a hackney-coach
they drove together to a young ladies' school in the suburbs,
where, after a short delay, a little girl appeared whom
Dick greeted with such tenderness that Mrs. Steele was
constrained to ask him if the child was his. With a grave
frankness Dick answered that she was. And then, after the
slightest pause, Mrs. Steele said gently: "I beg that she
may be mine too", and with her large-hearted human

understanding took the child home with them and treated her as their own.)

At the time, however, Dick's underlying sense of his own moral shortcomings asserted itself strongly; and, as a sort of private confessional and manual of morality, he began, with a curious seventeenth-century anticipation of Buchmanism, to compile a secret record of his misdoings and consequential contrition, "with the design principally to fix on his own mind a firmer impression of virtue and religion in opposition to a stronger propensity towards unwarrantable pleasures". Dick was no Uriah Heep, but naïvely sincere, like so many of his clever countrymen. He had no hesitation in openly acknowledging his faults, and, while never morbidly introspective, was candidly conscious of his religious imperfections. ("Dear good faulty Steele!" was to be Landor's comment on his character.) A dual impulse of literary satisfaction with its style and of a frankly contrite desire to stand in a white sheet *coram populo*, led him to publish the book in April under the title of *The Christian Hero* 'by Captain Richard Steele', with a dedication to Lord Cutts dated "Tower Guard", March 23, 1701, and a preface in which he commends the book to "his fellow Soldiers (to whose service more especially I would direct any thoughts I was capable of) hoping they would form to themselves, if any do not, a constant reason of their actions". In the *Spectator* he afterwards explained that the book had been written on occasions when he was Duty-Officer on Guard; "when the mind was perfectly disengaged and at leisure in the silent watch of the night to run over the busy dream of the day". Some cynic subsequently wrote that it was "dated from the Tower Guard as a present to the author's Colonel, that the Colonel might think him even in time of duty a very contemplative soldier; and, I suppose by the roughness of its style, he writ it there on the butt end of a musket!" The confessions and idealistic meditations of a smart Guards Officer created, as well they might to-day, something of a sensation: within three months the book ran into two editions, and a third was printed some years later. The sword had brought trouble to Steele in his duel with Kelly, but the pen was again asserting itself as his most effective weapon. Among the Wits, however, and his brother Guardsmen he "found himself slighted instead of being encouraged for his declarations as to religion; and that it was now incumbent on him to enliven his character; for which reason he was impelled to write a comedy called *The Funeral*, in which (though full of incidents that move laughter) Virtue and Vice appear just as they ought to. Nothing can make the Town so fond of a man as a successful play." And in that there is more than a hint of Dick's growing friendship with the brilliant Congreve—late of Trinity, Dublin, but then a Commissioner of Hackney-coaches—whose *Way of the World* had been played to crowded houses in the preceding year. *The Funeral, or Grief à la Mode* seems an odd title for a sprightly 'Comedy with Music', written by a Noel Coward of the period, but it adequately expressed the *motif*, which was a satirical attack on lawyers and undertakers, the mockery of grief and the mockery of justice;

stressing the contrast between Vice and Virtue and the
deference in which the author held all women. There was,
too, a soldiering episode in Act IV, with a squad of comic
recruits; but here Dick took the opportunity of registering
an Officer's admiration of the 'other ranks' of the Army.
'Matchlock'—a name he was to use again with 'Major
Matchlock' in the *Tatler*—was a soldier who had saved his
Officer's life at Steinkirk but at home had been man-
handled from constable to constable all the way up to
Town from Cornwall: "Yet, after all," says Trim, "'tis
upon the necks of such scoundrels as these gentlemen that
we great Captains build our renown". A similar appreciation appears in the *Tatler* (No. 87), in a letter purporting to
come from a Sergeant Hall at Mons, addressed to a brother
sergeant in the Coldstream and testifying to the gallantry
of the men in action there—like so many written by
British Officers from the same place two centuries afterwards. And 'Bickerstaff' adds—"For me, who knows very
well this part of mankind, I take the gallantry of private
soldiers to proceed from the same if not a nobler impulse
than that of gentleman and officers". The bravest man, he
asserts, "is a man of great courage and small hopes". And
again, in the *Englishman* Steele wrote—"I have marched
with 50,000 valiant men in my lifetime". His kindness of
heart, indeed, embraced all his subordinates while in the
Army—even old Mrs. Maplesden, the caterer at the Tilt-
Yard Guard at Hampton Court; for whom, after leaving the
Coldstream, he wrote a 'character', certifying "to whom
it may concern, that Margery Maplesden hath behaved

herself justly, modestly, and well; and that we do not know of ourselves, or have heard or believe, that she hath imposed upon any Officers or soldiers of either of the regiments of Guards or others".

In October 1701 he took his play to Christopher Rich, the manager of Drury Lane, who at once accepted it and put it in rehearsal with Colley Cibber and Nance Oldfield in the two leading parts. Dick was delighted, and invited all his brilliant friends to the First Night in November—wits and warriors, men-of-letters and women-of-fashion, including the Duke of Ormonde, the Duke of Devonshire, who was William's Lord Steward, and Arnold Joost Van Keppel, Earl of Albemarle, the King's closest friend and Colonel-Captain of the 1st Troop of Life Guards, together with his Countess, to whom, when he published it in December, Dick with his usual adroitness dedicated the play. And, as he had hoped, one or all of these latter must have commended it to the King; for in William's last-used memorandum book appears a scribbled entry of the name of 'Captain Steele', with a note appended "to be provided for". ("Ah! Dick Steele knew Life!"—as Hull the actor-poet wrote in his *Epilogue* to the play.) The first night was a *furore*, and Drury Lane was packed to capacity during a lengthy run. It was left to Captain Harry Graham, more than two centuries later, to follow Steele's example as a Coldstream Officer capable of writing brilliant *libretti* for successful comic operas.

III

THE 34TH AT LANDGUARD FORT

This is to certify that the bearer has served in that Company
of Her Majesty's Regiment of Foot commanded by the Right
Honourable the Lord Lucas whereof I am Captain, and that
I do hereby discharge him from the same for his better provision and advancement. As witness my hand and seal,

RICHD. STEELE

Discharge paper, *Landguard* 1703

ON March 8, 1702, 'the little gentleman in black velvet'
had driven his fatal mine at Hampton Court, and with
muffled drums Dutch William in his turn made his last
journey in State to Westminster. But not long before his
death he had made considerable additions to the strength
of the Army; and among the new units then formed was
the 34th Regiment of Foot (now the 1st Battalion of the
Border Regiment). In February His Majesty's commission
had issued to "Robert, 1st Baron Lucas of Shenfield,
Essex", then Lieutenant-Colonel in the 13th (later the
Somerset) Light Infantry, appointing him Colonel of the
new corps, which he was also directed therein to raise.
Lord Lucas was a personal friend of the King, with whom
he had served in Ireland and in Flanders, and at that time
was away from his regiment serving as Governor of the

Tower—where Steele was still on Detachment from the Coldstream. Lucas was allowed a certain latitude in the choice of his Officers, subject to a list of names compiled by the Earl of Marlborough, then Captain-General. At the time, Dick Steele was once more up to his ears in monetary difficulties. The life he had led in the Coldstream and the expensive society that he frequented were crippling him financially, and his literary earnings were a drop in the ocean of his debts. He was menaced with the Marshalsea: for many writs were out against him, and he had borrowed money heavily. The prospect of active service with a marching regiment—especially with a new one raised, as it would seem, to march with Marlborough against the French—appeared less remote than in the Household Brigade, and a campaign would afford him an opportunity both to dodge his creditors and to fortify his credit, perhaps, by conspicuous service and accelerated promotion. At that moment, at any rate, both weapons having proved equally precarious in financial results, the sword seemed to offer greater advantages than the pen. Once more, a decision rapidly arrived at was as quickly acted on. A word to the Governor, with whom he was on the friendliest terms, and Captain Steele's name was added to Lucas's list of Company Commanders for the 34th. As soon as his transfer was gazetted, Dick's fine Guards' uniform was sold to satisfy his creditors, and its former wearer, now in the more sombre livery of the Line, was hastening down to Colchester with Lord Lucas to start recruiting. For the men were to be raised in Essex and Norfolk on an establishment of twelve companies—each of three officers and sixty-six N.C.O.'s and privates; and one half-battalion was to be formed in Colchester, the other at Norwich. Dick was soon busy with his Colonel in the Town Hall at Colchester, attesting yokels and sending them to be armed and equipped by the Regimental Quartermaster, while outside in the Market Square drums rolled and fifes shrilled behind the beribboned sergeants. The men poured in at once; for it was rumoured that Ormonde, like Drake in earlier days, had been ordered to 'singe the King of Spain's beard' at Cadiz, and Marlborough, returned to power and popular favour on the Queen's accession, was known to be busy preparing for a new French war—which was destined to win lasting victory for his country and a Dukedom for himself. And as soon as both wings of the regiment were recruited up to establishment, the orders to move arrived. 'The route' had come, but it did not lie in the direction of the seat of war. Fate seemed relentless in her determination that Dick should never smell powder.

Only seasoned troops were to accompany Marlborough to Holland or Ormonde to Spain; and the 34th were raw. Weeks would have had to be spent in intensive training before the men could be even fairly efficient in their respective tactical capacities as musketeers, grenadiers, and pikemen. Seven companies of them, therefore, were ordered to the Tower, to take over from the Coldstream and be trained in garrison; and the remaining five were sent to the forts at Landguard, Tilbury and Sheerness, to relieve the veteran Buffs who were to form part of Ormonde's

Spanish Expeditionary Force. And so, with the larger wing, Lord Lucas found himself back again in the Tower, while poor Dick Steele, at the head of a rabble of greenhorns (how different from his smart company of Coldstreamers!), trailed a despondent pike along the road from Colchester to Landguard.

*　　*　　*　　*　　*

The fortress where Steele was to be stationed for the first—and last—time out of London was situated on the tip of the marshy promontory which divides the Stour and Orwell estuaries, with Harwich lying to its south-west across a mile of water. It was then a strong four-bastioned work, with batteries of 'cannon-of-emplacement'—which at the time were considered formidable—and accommodation for an infantry company of some 66 men, besides quarters for a Lieutenant-Governor, a 'Marshal', and a full complement of gunners, storekeepers, and boatmen. The Lieutenant-Governor at that time was a Colonel Jones, who found himself comfortable enough there as long as he could grant himself extended periods of leave in London. For a time Steele lived in quarters in the fort, but later, when the training of his men had been completed and he required congenial surroundings for the resumption of his literary labours, he got leave to live out in comfortable farmhouse lodgings at Walton, not far distant. All through the summer he was hard at work turning ploughboys into something like soldiers, and in the autumn was much bothered by a suit in the Chancery Courts, which he had

D

to bring by reason of an imbroglio about a bond into which
he had been led by Kelly, his Hyde Park antagonist, and
some unscrupulous blackmailing ladies of his acquaintance
of the name of Moore. The action petered out in the end;
but the lawyers would not let him alone, and all the succeeding winter he was worried with writs by creditors and
tradesmen. He had battles, too, with 'Higher Authority'
on the subject of his men's accommodation; for, having
been (though as a Cadet) in the ranks himself, Steele was
always a good regimental Officer and solicitous for the
welfare of his subordinates.

His protests were justifiable, for the fort at Landguard
was disgracefully ill-found and insanitary; and with the
sanction of Colonel Jones, who would appear to have been
less careful of the men's comfort than his own and quite
content to leave such details to an underling, he was constantly agitating for barrack improvements.

In September 1702, with the winter before him, he
wrote a strong official remonstrance to the 'Q' authorities
on the condition of the fort:

"The Governor of this garrison, Colonel Jones, *before
he went to Town, where he is at present*, directed Mr. Hub-
bard, your officer here, to represent the ill-condition the
barracks and all parts of this garrison are in, as to our
windows and tiling. There are sick men here of the
Company (whereof I am Captain) lying in their beds
exposed to all the injuries of the weather: I have at
present two sergeants, two corporals and nine sentinels

34

so ill that they cannot do duty, which, if I cannot attribute to this cause, I may say I do not expect the continuance of other men's health if the remedy be deferred until the winter advances further upon us. I hope my duty to them has not pressed me beyond rules to you in giving you this trouble.

"I am, Gentlemen,

"Your most obedient and humble servant,
RICHD. STEELE"

But 'Boards' are naturally wooden, and inspecting Officers proverbially short-sighted. The defects were tinkered at, but not repaired. In despair Dick appealed successfully in 1704 to his friend John Ellis, M.P. for Harwich and elder brother of Dr. Welbore Ellis his old Oxford tutor and Chaplain in the Life Guards, and then Under-Secretary of State; to whom he wrote gratefully, "It is a very signal service to this place that you are doing in relation to the sick soldiers, and don't doubt but they will appreciate it as such". In circumstances like these, it was not unnatural that desertions should be frequent, and much of Dick's time was occupied in correspondence with the Civil Power on the subject of apprehensions. In 1703 he had occasion so to write to John Caryll, Pope's friend, a J.P. in Sussex—"George Wilcocks, one of the fellows you brought from shipboard, a tailor, whose wife, as he told me in your hearing, keeps a brother's shop in Monmouth Street, deserted on Monday evening. Please do what you can to retake him." But Steele's good spirits and determination to get the best out of life did not desert him even in such depressing circumstances as those at Landguard; and he was constantly up in London for varying periods in the sympathetic company of his dear Joe Addison, now returned from his Continental travels and in rooms in the Haymarket. With Addison he joined the Kit-Cat Club—to which Jacob Tonson, Vanbrugh, Kneller, and most of their friends belonged,—which met at Christopher Catt's pie-house in Shire Lane by Temple Bar, and during the summer time in the garden of the *Upper Flask* tavern at Hampstead. Tonson built a room for the club in his country house at Barn Elms (now the Ranelagh Club), where portraits by Kneller of his brother members adorned the walls. On these long leaves in London, which grew more frequent as Steele's duties at Landguard gradually became less onerous and more in the nature of routine, he resumed his place in the Wits' circle at the coffee-houses and started a second play, *The Lying Lover*, dedicated (in desperation) to the Duke of Ormonde, which was produced by Rich at Drury Lane on December 2, 1703, after a revival of *The Funeral*. *The Lying Lover* was a sentimental adaptation of Corneille's *Menteur*, and introduced a scene at Oxford and one in Newgate Gaol which resembled the subsequent dramatic treatment of prison life by Gay in *The Beggars' Opera*. It ran for six nights only. Steele was dejected at the failure of his second comedy, and it was not until two years later that he finished another. He relapsed recklessly into his old extravagances, and dodged between Landguard and London beset by duns and bailiffs. The pen had failed him for the first time; it must be the turn of the sword again. The Duke of Ormonde, his original patron with the Life Guards, was back from Spain and now Lord-Lieutenant at Dublin. It was common talk at White's that he had been commissioned to raise a regiment of Dragoons in Ireland with himself as Colonel. In spite of dedications, and the constant advocacy of the unfailing Gascoigne, His Grace had done nothing for Dick since the cadetship. He might, however, relent so far as to give a commission in an Irish Cavalry regiment to a brother Irishman, which would neither commit him further nor cost him anything, though the additional pay meant much to Steele. After all, *on revient toujours à nos premiers amours*: Dick had begun his soldiering on a troop-horse, he might well continue it more successfully on a charger than in the 34th Foot. But it would all depend on a diplomatic and discreet approach to Ormonde. Uncle Henry was clearly no longer a dependable channel to the Duke's favour; but there was also John Ellis, M.P., a Minister, and still the *cher ami*, so gossips said, of the ageing Duchess of Cleveland. In March 1704 accordingly, he wrote a pressing letter to Ellis from Landguard, whither he had been ordered back from leave on a sudden scare.

But it was all to no purpose. The Duke proceeded with his recruiting in Ireland till June, and in July, when the establishment of the new regiment was completed, there was no troop left to be commanded by Captain Steele. All through these months, with his ears alert for some bailiff's knock on the door at any moment, Dick sat in his farmhouse-rooms at Walton enviously reading the accounts in the news-sheets of Marlborough's lightning triumphs on the Continent: of his combination with Eugene in June, his forcing of the Schellenberg in July, and, in August, of his decisive victory at Blenheim. The war seemed over and all hope of active service gone. He was disarmed. The pen was a broken reed, and the sword seemed equally unserviceable. With him there was nothing for it but to take to drink—or the 'occult sciences'.

IV

CAPTAIN STEELE 'FALLS OUT'

> As years came on I began to examine things and grew discontented at the times. This made me quit the sword and take to study of the occult sciences; in which I was so wrapped up that Oliver Cromwell had been buried and taken up again five years before I heard he was dead.   *The Tatler*, No. 89

DOWN a perspective of over two hundred years of great achievements and discoveries it is easy for us—who can learn more in a week from the scientific section of any Popular Educator than Hooke or Newton knew in all their lifetimes—to laugh at the research enthusiasms of amateur chemists in the early eighteenth century; especially when one, and the most attractive, branch of these dealt with the transmutation of metals. Alchemy, the mother of modern chemistry as surely as astronomy is the child of astrology, was not outside the purview of the old metallurgists, whose experiments sought the substance, spoken of as the 'Philosopher's Stone', which should purge the baser metals of impurities, leaving a substratum of pure gold. Since Charles II, accounted the most frivolous of our Kings, had proved that even a crowned comedian may found a Royal Society, Science had been fashionable: and in a capital where a Halley, a Hooke, or a Boyle were to be met out at dinner any evening, every gentleman of culture boasted a zeal for and a smattering in the natural sciences. Dick came to dabble in metallurgical chemistry by accident and as an anodyne. By chance, and most probably in a coffee-house, he met a man who interested him in the transmutation of metals, a subject in which, perhaps just because it was sneered at by his friend Swift as 'the Extraction of Sunbeams from Cucumbers', he affected an interest. A visit to the man's laboratory would seem to have convinced him that the chemist—or alchemist, if that term be more appropriate—was really on the verge of a discovery no more incredible than many of which the validity had been recently established. All that was wanted, of course, was money. Here was a chance! The crucible and alembic, after all, might be capable of producing at any rate a more tangible result in cash than the pen and sword. It was a gamble—not that a frequenter of White's would flinch from that—but it must be a gamble with someone else's money; for he had only his Captain's pay in the 34th, and that was mortgaged. It was at this juncture of affairs that he chanced to meet an old friend again—'Rivella'. Mrs. Manley was pleased to be interested and, because of her peculiar position in the London world and half-world, was enabled to help. She advanced some money herself and introduced him to another who lent a substantial sum: and Dick, so fired had his imagination become, began to negotiate for the sale of his commission. A room was hired in Poplar, where the necessary furnaces were built; and at the moment when all was prepared and paid for, Rivella, who had been put upon enquiry by rumours as to the chemist's *bona fides*, discovered he was a fraud. Dick was indeed in Queer Street. He was responsible to Rivella for her loan and for those she had procured for him; and these liabilities, added to those which he had incurred before, threatened to engulf him in the worst financial shipwreck of his career. His commission was still unsold and his pay was his sole sheet-anchor. Distracted by these reflections and Rivella's shrill reproaches, he sought refuge sometimes at Addison's rooms in the Haymarket, and sometimes at the house in Bond Street of a Lady Mildmay, one of his kindest hostesses, into whose society and that of her charming circle he fled to find distraction from his accumulated miseries. And he found it. Dick, as Rivella noted jealously, could be "the life of a party of ladies". And one lady, at any rate, at Lady Mildmay's made up her mind that life was not worth living without Captain Richard Steele. Margaret Stretch was no longer a girl; the daughter of a wealthy planter in Barbadoes and the widow of a colonist, she had a small fortune of her own, bequeathed her by a brother who had died while a prisoner on a French privateer. Amiable and warm-hearted, she fell deeply in love with Dick, who, at that crisis in his affairs, could scarcely reject so tender an opportunity of reclamation. He was not in love with her; yet he was profoundly grateful for the affection he had inspired in this woman, no longer youthful but sufficiently good-looking and with an assured position in Society (she was incidentally the aunt of Lady Cavan), who was willing to give herself and all she had to an insolvent Captain in a marching regiment. Rivella was furious, of course, and pursued him for years with a spitefulness which found its fiercest expression in a perversion of the truth about his career which she subsequently published in her *New Atlantis* (as quoted above). But the prospect which marriage with Mrs. Stretch held out, of liquidation of his liabilities, deliverance from duns, and from what he now admitted to be his servitude to the sword, decided him in her favour.

> Me Cupid made a happy slave,
> A merry wretched man;
> I slight the nymphs I cannot have
> Nor doat on those I can.
> This constant maxim still I hold
> To baffle all despair,
> The absent ugly are and old
> The present young and fair.

He would be free now to devote himself to what at last he recognized to be his real work in life—Literature. He was in his thirty-fourth year and his chances of promotion were nil; Lord Cutts had lost interest in him; and, to clinch the matter, Lord Lucas died in January 1705. Dick, who had been honestly attached to him, wrote a fine epitaph in Latin to his last Colonel, which ended—

INTER FORTISSIMOS LIBERTATIS EUROPAE VINDICES
LEGIONEM DUXIT.

After the funeral he sold his commission, handed over his company at Landguard to his successor, married his Margaret, and moved into a house she had bought in Westminster. And in April his third comedy, entitled appropriately enough *The Tender Husband*, was produced at Drury Lane. The sword had lost.

* * * * *

His retirement was not, however, to produce prosperity and an unruffled life for Steele. Fate continued her capriciousness and played cup-and-ball with him to the end. But somehow, after every tossing she allowed him to recover his position; except that all through his career, drink, debt, and defamation by rivals were his incessant enemies, with their concomitance of repeated lawsuits in which he rang the changes as plaintiff and defendant. In 1706 he was made salaried 'Gentleman-Waiter' to the Queen's Consort, Prince George of Denmark, but lost his delicate Margaret in the winter. She left him all her estate in the Barbadoes, and that same autumn he married her friend Mary Scurlock, his 'Dear Prue'; a woman of sterling worth whom he loved fondly and to whom he was comparatively faithful. Though Rivella sneered at her as 'a cried-up beauty' she was a pretty widow, who adored him though alive to all his faults, which he confessed to her quite freely, as a *Christian Hero* should:

"Prue, Prue, look a little dressed and be beautiful" . . . "Have settled the matter with Pother, who lends me the

money" . . . "If you can be so good as to forgive all that
is past, you shall not hereafter know any suffering from
indiscretion or negligence. I desire, my dear, that you have
naught else to do but *to be a darling*" . . . "I am, dear Prue,
a little in drink, but at all times your faithful husband"
. . . are a few extracts from his letters to her at varying
periods which tell their own tale. Well might she keep a
copy of the verses she wrote to him in the first year of their
marriage—

> Ah! Dick Steele, were I but sure
> Your love, like mine, would still endure
> That time not absence which destroys
> The cares of lovers and their joys
> May never rob me of that part
> Which you have given of your heart!

In 1707 Dick was made by Harley official 'Gazetteer',
at a sound salary; but on Prince George's death the following year his 'Waiter's' pay was replaced by a paltry
pension; and in consequence he took to the pen again—
with the result that he attained a lasting place among
the great masters of English prose. From its first issue the
Tatler took the country by storm, and its success, with the
help of Addison, continued unabated for two years. In
1710 Steele was appointed a Commissioner of Stamps, but
lost his Gazetteership for satirizing Harley. Next year he
started another success with Addison in the *Spectator*, and
afterwards with the *Guardian*, both of which publications
established their authors' fame. He was elected M.P. for
Stockbridge in 1713, and for Boroughbridge two years

later, when he was also dubbed a Knight; so that Prue, as
the wife of a man who "with the greatest justice gained
himself the applause of the best part of mankind", became My Lady. Steele never forgot, nor in his later days
regretted, his eleven years of soldiering. Allusions to his
experiences both in the ranks and as an Officer are frequent
in all his writing; and his portraits of soldiers—his *Sergeant
Hall*, his *Major Matchlock*, and his *Captain Sentry*, "a man of
good sense but dry conversation"—seem still to live. He
was slandered up to the end for his non-success in achieving active service; "for having", as Dennis wrote in 1720,
"in time of war taken pay for 20 (*sic*) years without being
in action: how could he be a hero who had never been
present at siege or battle?" And again: "All the world
knows that he served as a subaltern in the Guards for
bread". But such calumnies left Dick unharmed. It was no
fault of his that his sword had never been unsheathed save
on parade. He had three times changed his corps for
chances of so unsheathing it, which never came. And, all
along, as though conscious of its might, his pen had been
using his sword for its own peaceful but ambitious pur-
poses; that he might gain the position and experience
which would enable him at last to "write for the good
people of England" in such manner as would lead them to
forget the unsuccessful soldier in 'Isaac Bickerstaff' the
humorous philosopher, and the successful place-hunter
in 'Sir Roger de Coverley' the mirror of English squire-
dom. What ought to have been his epitaph was written
by a hostile critic in the *British Censor*, who, though

with quite another intention, anticipated the verdict of posterity:

> Once a Cadet, obscure and little known,
> Now such a bright conspicuous wonder grown.

For 'Dick'—the 'Private Gentleman Cadet', the Ensign, and the Captain—was never wholly extinguished in 'Sir Richard Steele'.

EDWARD GIBBON

Lieutenant-Colonel, SOUTH HANTS BATTALION,
THE HAMPSHIRE REGIMENT OF MILITIA

Captain—June 12, 1759
Major—1763
Resigned his Commission as Lieutenant-
Colonel Commanding—1770

In the Militia I was armed with Power . . .
GIBBON, *Autobiography*

(To the Tune of "Boyne Water")

To our Sacred King and his Counsellors
Our regiment was so praised:
In all the country, far and near,
Such troops could not be raised.
Then our route did come and off we marched
With honour still augmented,
And we left the camp at Winchester,
With our going sore lamented.

OLD MILITIA SONG

THE CAPTAIN OF HAMPSHIRE GRENADIERS

I

THE GIBBONS, MAJOR AND MINOR

*My principal obligation to the Militia was the making me an
Englishman and a Soldier.*   GIBBON, *Autobiography*

A POST-CHAISE lurched and laboured up the steep mountain road from the Lake of Geneva towards the French
frontier; and from its half-closed windows (for it can be
cold on the Jura even in late April) there came the sound
of subdued yet vehement conversation. Of its occupants—
three young gentlemen in the uniform of the Dutch
Army—two, obviously professional soldiers, were laugh-
ingly trying to allay the misgivings of the third, an un-
healthy-looking youth of one-and-twenty whose sallow face
showed a rather comic expression of mingled discomfort
and anxiety. The cause of the former was clear: for it was
the first time that Edward Gibbon had ever worn uniform,
and it was evident that the ill-fitting regimentals which
hung on him so loosely—except round the waist—were
borrowed plumage; while the latter was due to the situation in which he was placed as an exiled Englishman in
1758 trying to return home. The Seven Years' War had just
entered on its second twelvemonth; the road north through
Germany was one widespread battle-ground; and for a sub-

ject of King George II to risk travelling through French territory, even disguised as an officer of a neutral nation, was to court internment in a prison-camp if nothing worse. In voluble if slightly pedantic French young Gibbon was reiterating to his companions—two Swiss subalterns in the Stadholder's service, who had suggested the expedient and provided the uniform—his apprehensions of being stopped in spite of it by the frontier officials; and in that event, that he would only be exchanging the austere domesticities of Le Pasteur Pavilliard at Lausanne for even less comfortable accommodation in a casemate. For the French would show no mercy to an Englishman, so infuriated were they by Pitt's lavish subventions to Frederick of Prussia and the growing success of his forward military policy. (The elder Gibbon had only recently written to young Edward that Pitt's energy was increasing the British Army by many new units, of which one was now forming in Hampshire, to be called the 67th or South Hants Regiment-of-the-Line, and to be commanded by James Wolfe, a brilliant young officer of the 20th Foot; who had, however, just been given one of Amherst's Brigades and was off at once to Canada.)

At the Frontier post the chaise pulled up, and with whispered cautions to Gibbon to go on speaking French (which he did remarkably well, with a quite convincing Vaudois accent), the two Officers got out, followed by their masquerading comrade, whose fears, however, to his pleased surprise proved groundless. For the French officials—including the Lieutenant-of-Reserve on duty in a uniform which fitted even worse than his own—seemed quite unsuspicious, and after a perfunctory scrutiny passed their papers and seemed satisfied with their identities. Back in the chaise again, they rattled away with much whip-cracking and dust towards Franche-Compté and Lorraine, while the guards strolled towards the lonely estaminet to resume their denunciations of the perfidious English. And so the trio travelled safely on through the French fortress-towns and through Luxemburg into Holland, where Gibbon took leave of his companions (and his uncomfortable uniform) at Hertogenbosch, where they were in garrison, and proceeded by easy stages to The Hague and Harwich and thence to London, after an exile of four years, ten months, and fifteen days.

*   *   *   *   *

His father had come up to Town from Buriton to meet him. Their parting in 1753 had been a painful one; for young Edward had just been sent down from Oxford, then as tolerant of intemperance as it was intolerant in Theology, after his clandestine acceptance into the Roman Catholic Church. The fourteen months of his career at the University (to which he had gone up at fifteen, a ridiculously early age for any lad to assume the silk and velvet of a Gentleman Commoner) had been as great a failure as his previous two years at Westminster, with their frequent interruptions by his obstinate ill-health. In the Oxford of 1752 discipline was lax, and young Gibbon had spent as much time in truancy at Bath and London as he had in his

rooms in Magdalen: it was, indeed, on one of such sur-
reptitious *exeats* to Town that he had been received into
the Church of Rome by a Jesuit priest, Father Baker,
Chaplain of the Sardinian Embassy. The result was his
immediate banishment to Lausanne, where, in the house
of M. Pavilliard, a Calvinist *Pasteur*, he had recanted his
apostasy and laid the foundations of an amazing erudition
in Ancient History which neither Westminster nor Oxford
nor his perfunctory attendances at a succession of private
schools had been able to anticipate. Three important con-
siderations had moved his father to recall him; the first of
which was the dangerously disturbed condition of the
Continent and the peril in which his native country had
been placed by the disasters of the French War: the second
was young Edward's recently announced engagement to
Mademoiselle Suzanne Curchod, the clever and beautiful
daughter of another Calvinist *Pasteur*; and the third was
the fact that he himself had remarried during his son's
absence. His first wife had died in 1747 and he was not
unnaturally anxious that his heir, now twenty-one, should
meet, and commence an amicable understanding with, his
stepmother. On the way down to Buriton it can be
imagined that the father—cast by circumstances for the
part of the stern parent, but by nature an easy-going
sportsman and country gentleman—and the son, whom, in
character and tastes, long residence among foreigners added
to a studious and undeniably priggish disposition rendered
almost a stranger to him, had much to talk about. By the
time they reached Buriton Manor all constraint between

them had vanished; and after they arrived there the
second Mrs. Gibbon soon broke down her stepson's suspicious prejudice against her, and on his frank appreciation
of her "warm and exquisite sensibility" the childless stepmother and the motherless young man were not long in
adopting "the tender names and genuine characters of
Mother and Son". The Curchod affair was as satisfactorily
disposed of. Though Gibbon "sighed as a lover and obeyed
as a son" and broke off his engagement, he was not such
stuff as good husbands are made of. A "rational voluptuary", he was a vain and exacting egoist as well as a rapt
research student and scholar; and had he married Suzanne
she would have been an unhappy wife with Clio as an ever-
implacable rival. As it was, she accepted the severance with
what Gibbon believed to be "tranquillity and cheerfulness"; and six years later was happily married to her
capable and ambitious compatriot M. Necker, later Louis
XVI's Minister of Finance, by whom she had one child,
'Corinna', afterwards to grow into importance as Madame
de Staël. Gibbon and she continued on terms of friendship;
and in later years, much to the indignation of her friend
Rousseau, she was frequently his hostess in Paris. But
Edward's plans for the future were indefinite. His father,
impressed by his linguistic attainments and knowledge of
European thought, favoured the Diplomatic Service; while
his stepmother suggested legal studies and the Bar, laying
stress on the tranquil and scholarly attractions of the
Temple: advices his rejection of which he was in later
years disposed to deplore. Moreover the self-indulgent

youth and his tolerant seniors did not seem to think that there was any immediate need for him to settle down just yet, and the time passed agreeably enough at Buriton for the reunited family. His father drove them, behind a spanking team of bays, on visits to the neighbouring county gentry; he took them to see his horses run in the Hunters' Plate at Stockbridge; and tried to interest Edward in farming, the improvement of the estate, and the welfare of the tenantry. But Edward remained uninterested: nor would he handle a gun or mount a horse. He preferred the solitude of his study and the society of an ever-increasing battalion of books. There were, however, frequent visits to London—the London of Reynolds, Goldsmith, and Johnson—with parties at Lady Hervey's and the Mallets, and first-nights at Drury Lane where Garrick was then at his apogee. Young Edward also completed his earliest literary production—dedicated to his father—which he had roughed out at Lausanne and which he took down into Petersfield to be there translated into French by a Parisian captive in the Prisoners-of-War camp. (This, his first book, a slim duodecimo, was finished in six weeks: his last, the four volumes of the majestic *Decline and Fall*, was to take him twenty-two years.) Publication, however, did not follow until three years later, when Captain Gibbon was to present an advance-copy of his *Essai sur l'Étude de la Littérature* to the Duke of York:—the seed, it is to be feared, fell on exceptionally stony ground. The presentation took place, in fact, at a breakfast-party in the tent of Colonel Pitt, a kinsman of the Secretary-of-State, at

Winchester Camp—a place with which current events in Europe were soon to make the Gibbons, father and son, too closely acquainted for the peaceful continuance of their life at Buriton. Previously to young Edward's return from Switzerland the country had become gravely alarmed at the disasters of the French war and the disgraceful unpreparedness of the British Army, of which in 1756 only three regiments at home were found fit for service. The English contingents on the Weser and the fleet in the Mediterranean had both been forced to retire in face of the enemy. The safety of England was imperilled. Even Lord Chesterfield so far forgot Good Form as to cry despairingly "We are no longer a nation!" Too much reliance, so the country complained, had been placed on German mercenaries, such as the 7000 Hessians and Hanoverians then quartered at Basingstoke under a Count Justenberg. But whatever might be the condition of the troops on foreign service, the people and gentry of the English countryside were agitating for strong measures to enable them to fight, if necessary, for their motherland. Unlike the anti-conscriptionist democracy of a later and more enlightened age, the people were claiming the right of every subject physically fit to be allowed to qualify himself for the defence of his home. In consequence, the following year saw the passing of the Militia Act (30–32 Geo. II) which rescued 'The Old Constitutional Force' from the abeyance into which it had fallen since the Act of 1662, by which Charles II had remodelled it out of the County Trained-Bands. (The London Trained-Bands—now the Militia Battalions of the

Royal Fusiliers—were excepted, and survived long enough to allow *John Gilpin* to command a company in one of them.) Paradoxical though it may sound, the Militia was an actual 'Territorial Force'. As representing the Sovereign within the limits of their counties the Lords-Lieutenant were ordered to raise (by ballot) the County Militia regiments, to appoint appropriate Officers, and to sign their commissions on behalf of the King. The ballot took place almost at once in every county town, and the post was heavy with applications for commissions from the country squires and their sons, for the obligation of Militia Service was felt to be incumbent on every Gentleman of Position. In Hampshire the elder Gibbon had been one of the foremost agitators for the Act, and the younger, though by temperament and physique of unpromising military material, resolved to follow his father in patriotism, even if, as he admitted afterwards, he imagined that his patriotic duties would be conveniently local in character. Accordingly, the applications of father and son went in together to the Duke of Bolton at Hackwood Park, who, as Lord-Lieutenant of Hampshire, was also 'Brigadier-General of the Militia Forces' of that county. In due course they both received commissions, dated June 12, 1759, as Major and Captain respectively in the South Battalion of the Hants Militia Regiment.

And so it came about that Edward Gibbon the younger put on a second, and more comfortable, uniform.

II

FROM BOOKS TO BARRACKS

Amid the perpetual hurry of an inn, a barrack, or a guard-
room all literary ideas were banished from my mind.

GIBBON, *Autobiography*

> I was a plough-boy tall, sir
> My name was honest Dan;
> But at my country's call, sir,
> I've turned Militiaman.
>
> In regimentals bright, sir,
> Of scarlet I do shine,
> With hair tied-up so tight, sir,
> And whitened all so fine.
>
> And like a soldier prime, sir,
> I march both quick and slow;
> I stamp my foot in time, sir,
> And then kick up my toe.
>
> "DAN THE MILITIAMAN"

IN 1760 France was aiming at a descent on England and
the subjection of Hanover. In May of that year His
Majesty's Government having received repeated intelligence of actual preparations in the French ports for the
invasion of England, the Duke of Bolton received instructions to order the embodiment of the South Battalion of
the Hampshire Militia at Winchester. The time had come
for Major Edward to leave his hunters and his farm, and

57

Captain Edward his books. "It was too late to retreat and too soon to repent"; and so on June 4, Mrs. Gibbon waved farewell to her two warriors from the Buriton lodge-gates as they trotted away down the Winchester road, condemned, though then unconscious of their Fate, for the next two years and a half "to a wandering life of military servitude".

After a ghastly fortnight of the incessant work and worry involved in a sudden transformation by untrained officers and N.C.O.'s of a rabble of rustics into at any rate the outward guise of a disciplined regiment, the battalion, 500 strong, paraded on June 17 to march to Blandford, its first station. The Commanding Officer was Lieut.-Colonel Sir Thomas Worsley, a jovial but choleric baronet from the Isle of Wight, who, resenting interference by the Duke of Bolton, as titular Colonel of both the North and South Hants battalions, with the interior administration of his unit, had pulled such strings as he possessed to arrange for the regiment's being sent out of its own county into Dorsetshire. Edward Gibbon Senior was his Second-in-Command and Edward Gibbon Junior was one of five Captains. There were seven Lieutenants and seven Ensigns, an Adjutant, a Quartermaster and a Surgeon, with forty-two N.C.O.'s, fourteen drummers, and four hundred and twenty privates in seven companies of sixty men each (including one of Grenadiers). On the establishment of the period Field-Officers as well as Captains commanded companies, the Colonel's company being in charge of the senior subaltern, who ranked as a 'Captain-Lieutenant' accordingly: and both Field-Officers' companies carried colours.

The Officers seem mostly to have been of the fox-hunting, claret-swilling type of eighteenth-century country gentlemen, with more than one Tony Lumpkin among the juniors—scarcely congenial mess-mates to the reserved and fastidious Edward, whose temper was "insensibly soured by the society of our rustic Officers". But as Senior Captain and the Major's son, Gibbon was more closely associated with his seniors; and as the possessor of a methodical and precise mentality, was relied on to assist them and the Adjutant in such duties as the exercise of the Battalion and the drafting of orders:—surely the Battalion Orders of no regiment before or since can have been drafted in so sublime a literary style! With all reports and memos of a delicate or confidential nature in which precision and clarity of expression were required his help must have been invaluable.

The South Hants' uniform was similar to that of its Line contemporaries. Its head-dress, a tall conical cap, covered with fur in the Grenadier Company—which was shortly to be commanded by Edward Gibbon—with the royal cipher and the roses in front, surmounting the county badge of the Running Horse. (It was the only Militia regiment except the York and Lancaster that was privileged to wear the royal roses of red and white as its emblem.) Its scarlet coats were faced with yellow, and the men wore black stocks and gaiters, with buff breeches, a white shoulder-belt and cartouche-pouch, and a knapsack. The Officers wore swords and silver lace, a brass gorget when on duty, a red-and-silver waistcoat, white kerseymere breeches and white stockings with black garters. All ranks wore powdered hair and pigtails. The arms were flint-lock muskets and bayonets, and the Sergeants carried halberds. (How long and lovingly did the British Army cling to its association with muskets! It was not until the Great War of 1914–18 that the word 'Musketry' was supplanted by 'Small Arms' in the official manuals.) The men in the ranks were hinds and ploughmen, cottagers and small yeomen, with the fine physique of the Hampshire peasantry; and their self-respecting habits exacted less strict a discipline than that of the Regulars, who, apart from their fighting merits, were mostly jailbirds and the 'bad boys' of families. Most disciplinary offences among them rose from drunkenness—a failing which, translated from terms of beer into those of claret, they shared with their Officers and the professional classes. Gentle and simple alike, the Hampshire men had obtained the practical operation of the Act they asked for; but they were not quite sure at this stage of it whether soldiering should be treated as a patriotic gesture or a joke. Such was the composition and appearance of the South Battalion of the Hants Militia on June 17, 1760, when, headed by their drums but with a shockingly ragged civilian step, they marched away westward from Winchester with the greatest of English historians at the head of his company.

Of Blandford, a popular station with an alluring and hospitable choice of country-houses for the Officers and public-houses for the men, Gibbon wrote: "I hardly took a book in my hand the whole time there. The first two

months at Blandford I might have done something, but
the novelty of the thing, of which for some time I was so
fond as to think of going into the army, our field-days, our
dinners abroad and the drinking and late hours we got into,
prevented any serious reflection." In spite of drinking and
dinners the time passed strenuously enough in intensive
elementary training (for the Officers had to train themselves in order to train their men) and the establishment
of a proper disciplinary and administrative system: the
result of which was obvious when the Battalion took the
road again on August 22, bound for Hillsea Barracks,
Portsmouth—a station in its own county and, according to
Gibbon, "a seat of disease and discord". The first defect
was attributable to the dilapidated and insanitary condition of the barracks, and the second to the fact that the regiment, then less than three months old, had to be broken up
to furnish detachments at Porchester and Gosport Hospital,
where the men had exceedingly disagreeable duties as
guards and orderlies. But in September some companies of
the North Hants Battalion were ordered from Winchester
in relief, and in the succeeding month the rest of the
sister regiment arrived, and with the South Hants moved
out to camp on open ground for a few weeks' field-work
while the barracks were reconditioned. The North Hants
Militia had been embodied much earlier than the South,
and, as sometimes happens with near relatives, jealousy and
a sort of sisterly petulance disturbed the concord which
should have existed between the two Hampshire corps.

The North Hants claimed precedence as the elder sister,

for they had been embodied nearly six months earlier, and
were by now an effective and disciplined formation; moreover their leading Company was styled 'The Duke's
Company' and was nominally commanded by the Duke of
Bolton, Colonel, in virtue of his Lord-Lieutenancy, of both
battalions of the County Militia. Their Commanding
Officer, Sir John Cope of Bramshill, was as irascible as his
brother C.O. of the South Battalion; and both felt that
there was as little room for two kings in Hillsea Camp as
there used to be in Brentford. The War Office, however,
settled the dispute by ordering the South Hants to Maidstone, whence Major Gibbon took two companies on
detachment to guard French prisoners at Sissinghurst in
Kent, where they relieved the Buffs. The following month
the whole battalion moved into winter quarters at Dover,
with a detachment at Deal; and this station, the nearest to
the enemy that he was ever to attain, proved pleasant to
Captain Gibbon, now commanding the Grenadier Company, the personnel of which all came from the Alton
district: for though within eighty easy miles of London and
the librarians he could actually "exercise his men in sight of
the Gallic shores". He had leisure, too, to read again; and
in his quarters after tattoo could have a quiet hour with
Tully or Beausobre and "taste the pleasure of thinking".
Here Sir Thomas took two months' leave, and in his
absence Major Gibbon commanded, with Edward, the
Senior Captain, as his Acting Second-in-Command. However uncongenial his comrades or distasteful his duties may
have been to Gibbon he undoubtedly took his soldiering

very seriously. Completely devoid of any military instinct or experience, while he may have "sighed for his proper station in society and letters", he yet worked hard to teach himself the technical side of his profession, in which it was his business to instruct his men; and at a time when the tactical duties of infantry had changed in few essentials through the Middle Ages and the long seventeenth-century campaigns from those which prevailed under Belisarius and Narses, his classical erudition sharpened his growing zeal for proficiency in the control and command of men in action, just as the handling and instruction of his company gave him "a clearer notion of the phalanx and the legion". Field training, too, afforded him the healthy excitement obtained by his brother-Officers from field sports—"except", he wrote, "that I hunt with a battalion instead of a pack"; and the incessant round of active duty in the open air improved his health incredibly. Only during this period in his life was his gluttony a natural one: he had to earn his meals, and the sickly youth of some months since was transformed into as near an approach to a hard-bitten Infantry Officer as his comrades could imagine or believe. He might have resigned when the first scare of invasion had subsided; but he admits that his own keen-ness no less than "the friendly entreaties of the Colonel and the parental authority of the Major" prevented his doing so.

Decidedly, his Militia service was making a man of Gibbon.

III

FOLLOW-THE-DRUM

A wandering life of Military servitude.—GIBBON, *Autobiography*

When I see all the Captains on parade in their array,
When the drummers all are beating and the fifers sweetly play . . .
OLD MILITIA SONG

BUT in a marching regiment "bugles are always startling one into activity!" as a sedentary subaltern once protested to his Adjutant; and after six months in garrison at Dover the South Hants were on the march again in June 1761: this time to Winchester Down, where, with the 34th Foot and half a dozen other Militia battalions, they were to form part of Lord Effingham's composite Brigades. This four months' field training is described enthusiastically by Gibbon as "the most splendid and useful scene of our life. The consciousness of defects was stimulated by friendly emulation. We improved our time and opportunity in field days; and at the General's reviews the South Hampshire were rather a credit than a disgrace to the line." (How different from the peevish plaints of Blandford!). He had been home on leave at Buriton in the spring, where he had written an essay on Charles VIII of Naples; and, again in August, when he had begun a biography of Sir Walter

64

Raleigh. But leaves of a military nature pass too quickly
for the production or the turning-over of those of another
sort; and even the libraries of the Cathedral and the College, over which the camp looked down at the Itchen,
could not be visited with much profit during so strenuous
a period of training. Gibbon confesses, however, that
"amid the tumult of Winchester Camp I sometimes
thought and read in my tent"; and it was here that he
impressed the guests at a breakfast-party in Colonel Pitt's
marquee by presenting the Duke of York with an advance-
copy of his first published work.

The inter-regimental emulation mentioned by Gibbon
as being bred in the Brigades at Winchester included the
smartness and deportment of the individual soldiers as
well as their combined competition on parade and in the
field. With an eye on the next battalion, men shaved more
carefully, heads were powdered, queues plaited, with more
precision, and uniforms and equipment were more religiously cleaned. Efforts were even made to break the
Militiamen of their marked disinclination to 'pay proper
compliments' on guard or off duty to any Officers other
than their own, who, after all, in Civil life were the
'Quality' of their own countryside. The ritual of a military
salute in 1761 verged on the elaborate, and must have been
by no means easy to acquire among men who, as civilians,
were accustomed merely to grab off their hats and touch
their forelocks to their betters. The modern hand-salute
had not yet been invented, and old Orders of the period
prescribed that:

1. A soldier *not* carrying arms and meeting an Officer will, just before he comes to him, take off his hat *with spirit*, bring it quickly down the length of his arm, and, holding up his head, look full at the Officer till he passes. On no account is he *to bow* his head.

2. A soldier carrying a firelock and meeting an Officer is to pay his respects by immediately Shouldering and Carrying his arms and slowly marching on till he has passed him: if the soldier is standing, he must at once Shoulder and front the Officer and stand fast till he is passed.

3. No soldier is to touch his hat to an Officer when in the ranks or under arms.

Esprit de corps was even pushed as far as a rivalry between regiments in temperance and the cessation of profanity. As a contemporary canteen-poet claimed for the perfect Militiaman:

> He counts it quite a shame, sir,
> To hear a soldier swear;
> 'Tis what King George would blame, sir,
> No doubt, if he were there.
>
> Nor should he show his spunk, sir,
> By turning jolly fellow;
> He never will be drunk, sir,
> Nor even rather mellow.

But, alas, the bard sang more satirically than he intended, and the attempt to reclaim these hearty sinners showed no lasting result—if an ironical epitaph in the Close at Winchester of a Hampshire Grenadier whose conversion to small beer some three years later resulted fatally, is admissible in evidence:

IN MEMORY OF

THOMAS THETCHER

A Grenadier in the North Regt.

of Hants Militia, who died of a

Violent Fever contracted by drinking

Small Beer when hot the 12th of May

1764.   Aged 26 years.

*   *   *

Here sleeps in peace a Hampshire Grenadier
Who caught his death by drinking cold small beer.
Soldiers, be wise from his untimely fall,
And when you're hot, drink strong or none at all.

It is true that this virtuous casualty was a North and not a South Hants Militiaman; but there was a detachment of his regiment in Winchester Camp in 1761 and he was at any rate a Hampshire Grenadier, whose sad fate is indicative of what might have happened in the sister battalion had the emulation then extolled by Gibbon been carried to the same dangerous extreme.

*   *   *   *   *

But when the Harvest Furloughs were over—in these rural regiments as many men as could be spared were sent home annually during the Harvest months—the tents were due to come down with the autumn leaves; and in late October the battalion was ordered to winter quarters at

Devizes, whither it marched on October 23, covering the thirty miles over bad roads in a single day. After the hustle of Winchester the winter passed comparatively quietly: Gibbon took comfortable private lodgings and sent for books. "Nothing", he noted, "could be more uniform than the life I led there. The little civility of the neighbouring gentlemen gave us no opportunity of dining-out; the time of year did not tempt us to any excursions round the country; and at first my indolence and afterwards a violent cold, prevented my ever going to Bath." (His regret in not having visited Bath arose from recollections of his boyhood; for it was there that a private tutor first introduced him to Horace. And now, after fourteen years . . . "On every march Horace was always in my pocket and often in my hand.") "I believe in two months", continues his Devizes entry, "I never dined-out or lay from my quarters. November and December were indeed as much my own as any time can be while I remain in the Militia; but still, it is at best not a life for a man-of-letters." In the following February the training season began again, and the regiment was moved to its old quarters at more hospitable Blandford; where Gibbon's military enthusiasm, revived by field-work, impelled him to apply for a Staff billet as Brigade-Major to Lord Effingham, his General of last year at Winchester: "a post", he confided to his diary, "that I should be very fond of and for which I am not unfit". The non-success of his application seems to have somewhat damped his zeal; for in the entry of May 8, his twenty-sixth birthday, he pro-

tests that his temporary situation in the Militia, though
he endures it with spirit and application, is both unfit for
and unworthy of him.

At the end of May the South Hants again returned to
their own county and went into camp at Southampton,
then a fashionable resort. And the ballot of that summer
having produced some exceptionally fine drafts of recruits,
the old hands were free to enjoy a period of comparative
leisure while the energies of the Battalion staff were devoted to elementary instruction. The Grenadier company,
being fully trained, was not concerned with these activi-
ties, so its Captain went home on leave; for he felt he had
earned "two or three months of literary repose". Once
more in the library at Buriton he turned to Greek, which
he had not touched since reading it with his Swiss Pasteur.
But the idea of a history was ripening in his mind, and,
abandoning his Raleigh project for a more extensive
scheme, he began to elaborate some notes on the Republic
of Florence. He soon found, however, that the available
material was inadequate, and chafed for the freedom which
disembodiment would bring to travel in search of original
texts. Back again at Southampton, he found the recruits
had justified expectations and come quite marvellously to
hand. The student was once more extinguished in the
Senior Captain. He was proud of his corps: "we renewed
our vigour and youth, and had the Militia (embodiment)
subsisted another year, we might have contested the prize
with the most perfect of our brethren".

IV

LODGING THE COLOURS

I am glad the Militia has been, and glad that it is no more.

GIBBON, *Autobiography*

> The French came not, and if they had
> We should have had more glory.
> If they had made their landing good
> I could tell a better story.
> But they steered off and sailed away
> Repenting of this error,
> Because we bold Militia boys
> Inspired them all with terror.

OLD MILITIA SONG

THE victories that preceded Pitt's fall, and the peace prospects and slackening of war tension that followed it, produced an atmosphere of enervation in the training of the troops and of relief and frivolity in civilian society. As a soldier Gibbon deplored the first, and as an intellectual and a *gourmet* whose only social relaxations were talk and dining-out, he despised the second—which, as in 1919, expressed itself mainly in terms of dancing and drinking. The Southampton Assembly-Rooms were crowded nightly, and a grand County Ball was held there on August 24, which he did not attend; "for", as he admitted, "the same reason as carried so many people to it was what kept me away—*I mean the Dancing*". With regard to drinking, the discipline of sobriety was relaxed with all ranks: the Mess was merry all day after the Colonel's return from a cure he had been undergoing for his gout, and long after tattoo roll-call "Sir Thomas kept still assuring us after every fresh bottle how infinitely sober he had grown". But the following day's entry in Gibbon's diary shows a rueful result on the morrow: "I felt the usual consequences of Sir Thomas's company, and lost a morning because I lost the day before". Worse orgies followed in September, when Colonel John Wilkes, F.R.S., Commanding the Bucks Militia which was in camp near by, came over to spend the night.

The future popular hero of 'Wilkes and Liberty'—who was to sit triumphantly with Gibbon at Westminster twelve years later, and who, according to Boswell, was the only man who could manage Dr. Johnson—was a member of the notorious Hell-Fire Club, the fraternity of St. Francis (Dashwood) which met for unholy rites at Medmenham Abbey and in the 'Cave' at West Wycombe on the Dashwood Estate. He had been inducted into this sodality by its founder Sir Francis Dashwood, later Lord Despencer, a brother F.R.S., Bute's Chancellor of the Exchequer, and his predecessor in the command of the Bucks Battalion. For the delectation of brother Hell-Firemen such as Bubb Doddington and Paul Whitehead (the Secretary), Wilkes used to bring with him to these orgies a baboon dressed up as Satan—or, as some averred with horror, Satan dressed up as a baboon—and the ritual of the brethren accorded with their motto, borrowed from Rabelais' *Abbaye de Thélème*, which may be adequately translated into more modern vernacular as "Do as you damned well please". Brother Whitehead, who lived to be painted by Gainsborough, died in 1774; and as a crony of its ex-Colonel, was accorded a military funeral by the Bucks Militia when he was buried in the Dashwood mausoleum at Wycombe, with the band and a firing-party in attendance and six of the Grenadier company as pall-bearers.

But, even unsupported by his Mephistophelian monkey, Colonel Wilkes, as a good Medmenham Franciscan, could more than hold his own with any three-bottle Hampshire Officers—even with the redoubtable Sir Thomas himself. He proved great company, however; according to Gibbon's journal: "I scarcely ever met with a better companion; he has inexhaustible wit and humour and a great deal of knowledge. He told us himself that in this time of public dissension he was resolved to make his fortune. Upon this principle he has connected himself closely with Lord Temple and Mr. Pitt, and commenced a public adversary to Lord Bute (then Prime Minister) whom he abuses weekly in the *North Briton* and other political papers in which he is concerned. This proved a very debauched day. We drank a good deal both after dinner and supper; and when at last Wilkes had retired, Sir Thomas and some others—*of whom I was not one*—broke into his room and made him drink a bottle of claret in bed." After which, it may be presumed, Sir Thomas left his brother C.O.—

with a career before him that was to embrace Outlawry, two expulsions from Parliament, and the Lord Mayoralty of London—to sleep it off.

In October Lord Effingham, the G.O.C., held a grand review of the South Hampshire Defence Forces, which marched past the General in column of companies in review order. How the Fates must have laughed! The Berks Militia was led past by its Colonel, "The People's Jack", who punctiliously saluted the emblem of Royal authority for flouting which he was to be sent to the Tower within a year; and the Grenadier company of the South Hants marched by behind the future author of the *Decline and Fall of the Roman Empire*! The troops made a fine appearance; but an examination of the field returns showed Gibbon that the number present was but a little more than half the total establishment. "I doubt", he commented, "whether a nominal army of 100,000 men often brings 50 into the field!" For the Grenadier company a turn of detachment duty at Gosport Naval Hospital followed; and their Captain had occasion to report "a trait which characterized admirably our unthinking sailors. At a time when they knew that they should infallibly be discharged in a few weeks, numbers (who had considerable pay due to them) were continually jumping over the walls and risking the losing of it for a few hours' amusement in Portsmouth!"

*   *   *   *   *

But the High Gods, and the lower pacificism of the young George III and Bute, decided that it was time for

Gibbon's active soldiering to cease. Pourparlers with the enemy had continued through the autumn, and at Fontainebleau on November the 3rd the Duc de Choiseul— with the languid approval of Madame de Pompadour and the violent disapproval of Mr. Pitt—signed the preliminary Treaty which was soon afterwards to be ratified by the Peace of Paris. In December came orders for Disembodiment; and the following letter from the War Office was read by its Captain to each company on parade in the presence of the Commanding Officer: "To Lieut.-Col. Sir Thomas Worsley, Bart., Commanding the South Battalion of The Hampshire Militia. Sir, The King having been pleased to sign an order for disembodying the Corps of Militia of the County of Hampshire under your command with all convenient speed, I am commanded by His Majesty in his name to convey to you the great satisfaction he has received from the seasonable and meritorious service of the Militia of that county. As a mark of his royal approbation I am commanded to acquaint you that His Majesty is pleased to permit each non-commissioned Officer and private man to keep his clothes and knapsack which are at present in wear, and also to allow them respectively 14 days' pay from the day of their being disembodied. Before disembodying you are to cause His Majesty's orders to be read at the head of each company in your corps, so that they may be conversant of His Majesty's gracious bounty to them. The good behaviour, activity, and zeal of the Officers and private men of His Majesty's Militia, exerted for the security and defence of this kingdom, obliges me at the same time to express the satisfaction I feel in having the honour to communicate to you His Majesty's gracious approbation of their service." (A communication in its phrasing not unworthy of Gibbon himself, and singularly similar in sentiment to that promulgated to the Militia's successors at the close of the World War a hundred and fifty-eight years later.) On December 17 the regiment broke up—or in more accurate military parlance, 'broke down'. Under the system of local balloting the men of each Militia company were recruited from the same district; and the personnel of the Major's company in the South Hants was drawn from Buriton and Petersfield, while the men of the Grenadier company were from the Alton area—though geographically this forms part of North Hampshire. But the actual siting of the separation-line between the ballot areas of the North and South battalions is uncertain. It would appear, however, from the enrolment records, to have formed an arc, running south-west from the Surrey border, through Basingstoke, Micheldever, and Winchester, to the edge of Wiltshire north of Romsey; for the fat sheep-lands and more fertile farms north of such an arc supported in the eighteenth century a larger rural population than the more sparsely peopled areas south of it. At any rate, Gibbon has left it on record that his Grenadiers were Alton men; and, amid the farewell cheers of their comrades, they marched off behind him as he followed his father's company along the homeward road through Alresford,—where they met a wing of the 14th Foot (now the

West Yorks Regiment) on its way from Dover to its peace-time station at Winchester. Its veteran commander, a Captain Meard, was, with his Officers, the guest of the Gibbons at supper, and "made the evening rather a drunken one". Next morning both bodies paraded to proceed on their diverse ways; and the contrast between the Regulars and the Militiamen warmed Gibbon's heart. "About the same hour", he exults, "our two corps paraded to march off; they (the 14th) an old corps of Regulars who had been two years quiet in Dover Castle; we, part of a young body of Militia, two-thirds of our men recruits of four months' standing, two of which they had passed on very disagreeable duty at Gosport. Every advantage was on their side, and yet our superiority, both as to appearance and discipline, was so striking that the most prejudiced Regular could not have hesitated for a moment." *Esprit de corps* was clearly still as strong in him as the spirit of personal freedom; but the latter prevailed as they approached the junction of the road with that which led to Buriton. It was exactly two years six months and fifteen days, by his own meticulous reckoning, since he and his father had ridden along that road to their first muster at Winchester. To many men the presence of a father as an immediate senior in the same corps would have been insupportable; but to the younger Gibbon it had been a reassurance and a solace. The cheerful heartiness and liberal spirit of his father ensured a confidant who, though he could not understand it, condoned with sympathy the petulant reserve and self-centred scholasticism of his son.

In fact, the Captain, with the fresher curiosity and adaptability of youth, became the better Officer of the two; though the Major, a soldier for the first time at fifty-three years of age, could claim an outward distinction of bearing and a bluff demeanour which accorded better with the King's uniform. But soldiering had drawn them closer together than domestic and civilian contact at home could ever have done, and a warm affection now united them. Arrived at the fork of the road near Ropley, the companies separated; the Major's breaking off southward, while the Captain headed his grenadiers north-east for Alton, where they spent the night, after drinking his health (at his expense) at tattoo roll-call. The final day of duty was spent in the business details of disembodiment—the adjustment of pay, back-pay, and deductions, the delivery-up and checking of arms and equipment, the filling-in of forms and rolls and papers. More beer and more cheers for the Captain and Lieutenant Harrison, his subaltern—whose family lived in Alton—and then each grenadier became once more a 'mucky civilian'. Gibbon put up for the night at the Harrisons' house, "where I was received with that old-fashioned breeding which is at once so honourable and so troublesome". And on the morning of Christmas Eve he was driven home at last by the Harrisons' coachman.

At Buriton the disembodiment of the Major's company was a matter of greater ceremony, as befitted his superior rank and dignity. On arrival at Petersfield he had handed over the company to Lieutenant Smith and hurried on ahead: so that, when his men marched into Buriton they found their commander waiting for them with Mrs. Gibbon and some of the local notabilities. Formed up before him, they fired three volleys of a *feu de joie*, after which the Major's Colours were 'lodged' in ceremonial form, the company drums were stored, and the N.C.O.'s and men, having handed in their arms, sat down to the plenteous dinner provided for them by the Major's lady. And when the beering and cheering at last were over "they separated with great cheerfulness and regularity".

In the tranquillity of Buriton Captain Gibbon sat down in the new year to review his experiences—"As this was an extraordinary scene of life in which I was engaged above three years and a half from the time of our embodying, I cannot take my leave of it without some few reflections. When I engaged in it I was totally ignorant of its nature and consequences. I offered because my father did, without ever imagining that we should be called out, till it was too late to retreat with honour. Indeed, I believe that it happens throughout, that our most important actions should be determined by chance, caprice, or some very inadequate motive. After our embodying, many things contributed to make me support it with great impatience. Our continued disputes with the Duke of Bolton, our unsettled way of life which hardly allowed me any books or leisure for study, and more than all, the disagreeable society in which I was forced to live. After mentioning my sufferings I must say something of what I found agreeable. Now that it is over I can make the separation much better than I could at the time. The unsettled way of life itself had its advantages. The exercise, and the change of air and of objects amused me at the same time as it fortified my health. A new field of knowledge and amusement opened itself to me, that of military affairs, which in my studies and travels will give me eyes for a new world of things which before would have passed unheeded. Indeed, in that respect, I can hardly help wishing our battalion had continued another year. We had got a fine set of new men; all our difficulties were over; we were perfectly well clothed and appointed, and from the progress our recruits had already made we could promise ourselves that we should be one of the best Militia corps by next summer; a circumstance that would have been the more agreeable to me as I am now established as the real acting-Major of the Battalion. But what I value most is the knowledge it has given me of mankind in general and of my own country in particular. The general system of our Government, the methods of our several Offices, the departments and powers of their respective Officers, our provincial and municipal administrations, the views of our several parties, the character, connections, and influence of our principal people, have been impressed on my mind, not by vain theory but by indelible lessons of action and experience. I have made a number of valuable acquaintances, and am myself much better known than, with my reserved character, I should have been in ten years passing my summers here at Buriton and my winters in London. So that the sum of all is that I am glad the Militia has been, and glad that it is no more."

The elder Gibbon resigned his commission almost immediately—which explains his son's allusion to holding acting-rank as Major. In plain terms Gibbon *père* was 'fed-up' with soldiering, and hungered for farming and his county life again, for his hunting and shooting and Quarter Sessions. He had, too, the greatest faith in his son's capacity to fill his place, and in due course the Senior Captain was gazetted Major and Second-in-Command to the evergreen and still convivial Sir Thomas. The regiment was not called out again for training for four years.

* * * * *

The new Major Gibbon lost no time in putting his country and his country's service behind him. Within six weeks of disembodiment he was in Paris, where he found the cooks and the books and the society of his former foes as congenial as ever. At the present day War is a menace to civilization because it has freed itself from the restrictions under which it was conducted in Gibbon's time. Now that it cannot but involve all the manhood and resources of a nation (unless, as seems not unlikely, huge conscript armies are replaced by small highly trained forces of technicians), it must be fought to the death—economic, social, and political—of that nation, and end in its collapse. But, in the eighteenth century, wars were fought with limited means for definite objectives. It was Napoleon who was later to destroy the condition of affairs that existed in Gibbon's day, whereby when two belligerent nations decided that the issues were not worth further sacrifices, they negotiated, and were prepared to accept the resulting treaty as a settlement by consent, involving no intolerable humiliation to any of the high contracting parties. Accordingly, Gibbon found the British respected by the French as recently formidable enemies but now reconciled friends, whose fashions and literature and even sports were everywhere popular. He went to the Opera and the play, dined with Madame Bocage and talked with Diderot and d'Alembert; and before he moved on to his beloved Lausanne had almost forgotten his grenadiers, the Gosport guard, and even the sour claret at Devizes. In Switzerland again, he revisited Voltaire and met John Holroyd—afterwards Lord Sheffield—who became his patron and his firmest friend, and in whose house he was to die. A man-of-the-world and a Sussex landowner who was to raise and command a cavalry regiment, Holroyd was also a writer and man-of-letters, with an attractive and sympathetic disposition. The two men became inseparable and went together on a protracted tour through Italy, where they made a field survey of the Genoa battleground and eventually arrived in Rome. And it was among the ruins of the Capitol on October 15, 1764, that Gibbon first projected the scope and plan of his great history "while the barefoot friars were chanting vespers in the Temple of Jupiter".

After two years of travel Gibbon returned, in June 1765, to Buriton, where and in London he passed the next five years. In the following May the South Hants Militia commenced the regular sequence of their annual Battalion trainings for twenty-eight days at Southampton, with Gibbon—now Lieutenant-Colonel—in command, owing to the death of old Sir Thomas Worsley. And he continued to command the regiment at every Battalion training until 1770. But in that year his father died, Buriton was sold up to clear the estate of debt and mortgages, and Lieutenant-Colonel Gibbon sent in his papers. During his period as Commanding Officer, whatever may have been his pride in his men's smartness and soldierly proficiency, his old dislike of the bucolic and alcoholic manners and habits of the Officers became intensified by the more "polished and intellectual society" to which by now he had become accustomed in London and abroad. In addition, he was far too much preoccupied with his heavy and exacting preparatory labours on the *Decline and Fall* to be able to spare a whole month each year for soldiering. And so, after holding a commission in the South Hants for eleven years, Colonel Gibbon dismissed the battalion for the last time —and consented to sit to his friend Sir Joshua Reynolds for the portrait in uniform of which a reproduction still forms the frontispiece of the most stupendous work of history in any language.

(Nine years later, another historian of eminence, though not of such surpassing greatness, commanded the Battalion. This was Gibbon's friend Lieutenant-Colonel William Mitford, who published in 1784, at his suggestion, a *History of Greece*. He joined as a Captain in 1771, and was the brother of Sir John Freeman Mitford, Speaker of the House of Commons and afterwards first Lord Redesdale.)

* * * * *

Edward Gibbon was a vain man, snobbish and pedantic, but possessed of a great brain and incredible powers of industry and application, which—though he might quite early have rid himself, as others did, of his military obligation—he devoted unreservedly, and in circumstances wholly uncongenial to himself, to the efficiency of his corps and his duties as an Officer. His personal pride may have been priggish and pragmatical, but he had pride of regiment as well. And as an acknowledgment of this inter-action of his dual personalities he has left it handsomely on record that "the Captain of Hampshire Grenadiers has not been useless to the Historian of the Roman Empire".

SAMUEL TAYLOR COLERIDGE

Private, THE KING'S 15TH LIGHT DRAGOONS
(now 15TH KING'S ROYAL HUSSARS)

"I sometimes", said Coleridge to a friend, "compare my own life with that of Steele (yet, O how unlike!) from having myself also for a brief time borne arms and written 'Private' after my name—or, rather, after another name."

Letters, Conversations, and Recollections
of S. T. Coleridge, i. 189

S. T. Coleridge

CANDLESTICK DUTY

I

RECRUITS AT READING

I see the youth, in my mind's eye I see him
Leap his black warhorse . . .

JANUARY—so History seems to show—is a month of inclemency, in politics as in weather, to kings; during which, in an atmosphere not usually associated with precipitancy, they are apt to lose their heads. For, as in the case of Charles of England a century and a half before, the roofs of his capital were rimed with frost when 'Citizen Capet's' last drive through Paris came to an end on January 21, 1793, amid the rolling of Santerre's drums on the Place de la Révolution, at the spot where the obelisk now stands, but where then stood the Guillotine. And eleven days later the drums rolled equally loudly in the same place after a Citizen-Crier had read the proclamation of War by the National Convention against Holland and Great Britain.

As was to be expected, Pitt took up the challenge eagerly; and the walls in English towns and villages were soon emblazoned with recruiting posters—each corps, as in the much later circumstances of Kitchener's Armies, devising and disseminating its own.

The distinguished regiment which is now the 15th

Hussars, but which was then the King's 15th Light Dragoons, or, as it was more popularly known, 'Eliott's Light Dragoons', at that time lay at Reading. (General George Augustus Eliott, K.B., the father of the 15th, was an Eliott of Stobs. A veteran of Fontenoy and Dettingen and of the capitulation of Havana—where his share of the loot amounted to £24,500—George III created him first Baron Heathfield of Gibraltar as a reward for his successful defence of the Rock against its four years' siege by the French and Spanish armies from 1779 to 1783. He died in 1790.) The Commanding Officer of the 15th had been warned in April to prepare four troops of seasoned soldiers and picked recruits for service in Flanders. These embarked in May, and were attached to Dundas's 3rd Cavalry Brigade at Tournai; and later, in August, a squadron under a Captain Pocklington was under fire between Le Cateau and Landrecies, on the same ground that, exactly one hundred and twenty-one years afterwards, was to be hallowed by the sacrifice of its successors. Meanwhile, these troops at the front had got to be fed with reinforcements, and recruits to be intensively trained as drafts. And so it came about at Reading on a bright morning in late autumn that Colonel Gwyn, the C.O. of the 15th, accompanied by his Adjutant and the more awful presence of a Squadron-sergeant-major, left his quarters to inspect a batch of newly enlisted recruits which had come in the previous evening.

Called to attention, the two ranks of 'rookies' did their trembling best to stiffen into soldierly semblance and so to present an earnest of their martial ambitions. But a yokel here and there forgot to spit the straw from his mouth, and some candidates from counting-house or counter shuffled their as yet undisciplined feet as the Colonel clanked slowly down the lines, asking an occasional question and examining each man's face and proportions like a fat-stock dealer at a cattle sale.

The men paraded had already been passed by the Medical Officer and had given their particulars and been attested in the orderly-room; so that the Colonel knew that each of them might now be regarded as an Eliott in embryo, and he rather welcomed their unpromising exteriors. "A good draft," he heard himself boasting later; "but Gad, sir! you should have seen them six weeks ago, before we'd begun to handle 'em!"

He came to a sudden halt, however, before the flank man of the front rank, a plumpish youth of some 5 feet 9 inches, who, with his peachy West Country complexion, unruly black hair, and large eyes of a mild but bewildered grey, looked younger than his one-and-twenty years. He was plainly, even a little shabbily, dressed, and his head hung down, so that the gallant ribbons tied round his hat by the Sergeant yesterday drooped limply to his shoulders.

"What's your name, my lad?" The head was raised, but the grey eyes blinked and the girlish skin blushed crimson. It was one thing to invent a false name on the spur of the moment and give it to a shirt-sleeved Quartermaster in a noisy office, but quite another to repeat the lie convincingly and in a listening silence to this tremendous inquisitor in full regimentals. Swallowing hard, and straining his mind to ensure an accurate recollection, the recruit replied, "Silas Tomkin Cumberback, sir." Neither the Oxford nor the Cambridge accent as yet had been invented; but the intonation of his voice, its precise and halting tenor and slightly precious evaluation of vowels and consonants, betrayed scholarship, bookishness, and all the unsoldierly qualities of a university runaway. The names were inventions. The surname he had noticed somewhere over a shop-door; though it also implied a jibe against himself, born of consciousness of his deficiencies as a horseman. The two Christian names he had selected at random; and of all three together the initials only were those of Samuel Taylor Coleridge, scholar of Jesus, Cambridge, Browne Medallist, winner of the University Greek Ode prize, and runner-up for the Craven to Butler of St. John's. (This was Samuel Butler, Headmaster of Shrewsbury from 1798 to 1836, and afterwards Bishop of Lichfield; the grandfather of Samuel Butler, of Shrewsbury and St. John's, author of *Erewhon* and *The Way of all Flesh*.)

A titter passed down the ranks of the recruits, either at the incongruous tone of the reply or at the faintly ridiculous sound of each of the three names; and the Colonel grinned sardonically as he went on to ask, "And what have *you* come here for?" A baleful flash from the Sergeant-major's eye elicited the answer, "For the same reason as most people come, sir; to be made into a soldier". The Colonel grunted; and after a practised and rather sneering scrutiny, enquired again, "D'you think you can run a Frenchman through the body?" The head jerked up, and with a little fire the answer came, "That I don't know, because I've never tried, sir; but I'll let a Frenchman run *me* through before I'll run away!" Colonel Gwyn laughed: he was plainly pleased. "That'll do," he said, and, turning, stalked down the rear rank with an order to his Adjutant to march the party over to the Quartermaster's to be fitted with uniforms.

II

AFTER 'LAST POST'

Turbulent, with an outcry in the heart
And Fears self-willed that shunn'd the eye of Hope,
And Hope that scarce would know itself from Fear;
Sense of past Youth, and Manhood come in vain.

OUTSIDE, the trumpets were blowing 'Last Post'. Sunk in
a heavy humour, Private Cumberback lay on his palliasse,
and the buzz of broad barrack-room talk from the men
around him allayed a little the vehemence of his vibrating
nerves and somehow deadened his sense of immitigable
misery. For his reflections on what he had done during the
past two days tinged the dull monochrome of his emotions
with a still deeper grey. His crushing disappointment at
not winning the Craven, the bar presented to his University ambitions by his total incapacity for mathematics,
and the continued harassing by creditors, had focussed the
whirl of his bitter thoughts into one dominant idea—
release by flight from Cambridge and all it stood for. Poor
lad, his mathematical incapacity extended to any compre-
hension of practical finance, and his chief creditor was a
furniture dealer, whose tout, two years ago, had been mis-
taken by the casual and improvident young freshman for
some underling of the Bursar's; with the result that the
insidious query, "How may I furnish your rooms, sir?"

had merely met with the answer, "Oh, just as you please!"
And the hundred pounds or so which stood at the foot of
the bill—many times rendered, and now at last with
threats—had come to destroy the sleep and peace of mind
of the simple son of the Vicar of Ottery St. Mary. As to
ambition, Butler and John Keate—Fellow of King's, afterwards Canon of Windsor, and later to be the famous
'Swishing headmaster' of Eton—had been above him for
the Craven, and of what use was ambition to him, the
ninth son of a country parson? Moreover, there was, of
course, a girl—Mary Evans, with whom he had been in
love since his school-days and who had proved unkind.
He had bought a lottery-ticket some weeks before, and the
draw was to take place in London in a few days' time. So
there followed the stealthy anabasis to Town, where he
dawdled until the lottery was drawn, praying desperately
and drinking recklessly to drown his piteous agony of
mind. He drew a blank.

It was the last straw. What happened during the succeeding miserable hours he could scarcely recollect: the squalor of
dissipation in stews and taverns, the *largesse* of his last coins
to other poor wretches tramping the midnight streets—and
at last the chance sight of a recruiting-poster under a flicker-
ing wall-lamp:

G. ♛ R.

WANTED

A FEW SMART LADS

FOR

THE 15TH (ELIOTT'S) LIGHT DRAGOONS

God Save the King!

Unlike his friend and fellow 'Blue' Charles Lamb, Coleridge had learnt at Christ's Hospital under the régime of Bowyer to loathe and fear discipline, and all his life he had hated horses and soldiers. But the ills of a mind like his, he thought, might be cured of all such prejudices by self-immolation. Souls greater than his had sought salvation in the stress of battle; and, after all, routine, the relief from material anxieties as to food and clothes, a bed, and pocket-money, the healthy fatigue of a round of daily duty, might all prove anodynes, harsh but effective, for such suffering as his. And so, as he read the poster with eyes that were hollow with traces of the struggle within him between the force of circumstance and the force of inclination, he grasped the nettle and went to the recruiting office; where he received King George's shilling from a kindly Sergeant, who lent him, in addition, half-a-guinea and sent him to some lodgings for the night. And then had followed the march through cheering villages to Reading, and his initiation as a Light Dragoon. Contrary to Coleridge's expectation, the doctor had failed to detect any trace of the chronic rheumatism which was his lifelong affliction, or of the neuralgia which accompanied it, and which was now splitting his head in two and was later to drive him to 'the Kendal black drop'—the deadly lenitive of opium. And now the poet-scholar of Jesus was turned into a Trooper; it was good-bye to his hopes and ambitions of a few days since; good-bye to the books, the prose, the poetry, philosophy, and metaphysics, which had meant Life to him since first he had learnt to read. He looked up at the sword and helmet, the belt and coatee and breeches, folded together neatly on the shelf above him with the spurred boots beneath, and he thought of the Scholar's gown and college cap hanging behind the door of his rooms in Jesus. He did not know much about soldiering, but he thought he would know how to die. He remembered Blandford's epitaph in King's Chapel—'JACTAT GENUS ET NOMEN INUTILE'.

The men had ceased to talk and the place seemed suddenly quiet and still. Relaxed by the extreme of mental and physical exhaustion, he sank back on the mattress. And over at the quarter-guard the trumpeter blew 'Lights Out'.

III

SILAS ON PARADE

> There was a time when, though my path was rough,
> The Joy within me dallied with Distress,
> And all misfortunes were but as the stuff
> Whence Fancy made me dreams of Happiness.

FOR all his bookishness and neurasthenic moods of introspection, Coleridge was a 'good mixer'. He possessed a
singular personal charm which throughout his life attached
to him all whom he met of every class and culture. He had
no *mauvaise honte*. He was ingenuous, sincere, and amiable;
talkative, even voluble, "a whirlwind in conversation"; he
loved the company of his fellow-men and was devoid of
the slightest trace of snobbery. A day-dreamer, he was
never aloof; an intellectual, he never obtruded his scholarship; unsophisticated, he yet could hold his own with
witty *ripostes* which would turn the laugh, however dis-
paraging, to his side. Though sensitive, he never bore resentment, and the rough, hearty banter of the barrack-
room passed him by. Lacking such qualities, he might
have become a butt. Possessing them, 'Silas', as the men
now came to call him, grew into an established favourite.
His awkward hopelessness at drill and in the riding-school,
which to another would have made life a hell at the hands

96

of instructors and jeering comrades, was looked on indulgently as part of a chaffing legend. Even roughrider and riding-master diluted their customary vitriol with a good-humoured playfulness. "Take care of that there Cumberback, he'll ride over you!" was the fiercest censure that would assail him as he was being bolted with through the files on some old rogue of a troop-horse with a mouth like iron, only to be scraped off against the top of the stable-door to an ecstatic chorus of "Silas is off again!" Pegasus, not a troop-horse, was his proper mount; and he could never sit a charger for long except the sheepiest on the roster. His grooming, too, was execrable—chiefly by reason of his rheumatism, which made stooping an agony. (On the wood of his horse's forage-rack in the stable he carved the words 'EHEU! QUAM INFORTUNII MISERRIMUM EST FUISSE FELICEM'.) It was the same with his arms and kit. "Whose rusty scabbard is this?" asked the Orderly Officer on his rounds one day, pointing to the offending sheath as it hung on the wall. "Is it a *very* rusty one, sir?" came in the now familiar tones of Private Cumberback. "Very rusty indeed!" said the Officer ominously. "Then it must be mine, sir," replied, with a sigh, the incorrigible recruit. He puzzled his comrades. They knew him for a gentleman, and wondered why one so militarily unhandy should ever have enlisted. Some talked of debts and the Fleet, others of a crossing in love or an undiscovered crime, and even of a cheating of the hangman.

The rumour spread that he was a deserter from the infantry 'hiding among the horses': this lent him a pro-

tective interest with the others, for if it could be brought
home to him it meant a hideous flogging. In 1793 discipline was brutally enforced, and any dereliction was
punishable with 'the black hole' or with lashes which
varied in number and severity according to the character
of the offence. For the ranks were filled with men from the
lowest classes and from the Civil prisons. But the other
recruits and troopers, while they jeered at his horsemanship, did Coleridge's grooming for him, and cleaned his
kit and equipment and masked his numerous and absent-
minded delinquencies. Bruised and aching from his falls,
he gratefully repaid them by writing their letters and, to
the best of his poor arithmetical capacity, casting up their
accounts—for most of his comrades were illiterate. Love-
letters were his *forte*; and many a wife or sweetheart of a
Light Dragoon must have marvelled at her receipt of some
sudden and inexplicable burst of amorous eloquence. That
Coleridge managed to win popularity among such men by
force of character and personality would by itself attract
the attention of his Officers, in spite of his naïve efforts
at obscurity and disguise. His Troop-leader, Captain
Nathaniel Ogle, had observed him closely during his
earlier period 'on the Square' and had marked him down to
be his orderly as soon as elementary training should be
concluded. He had taken the measure of Private Cumberback as being no ordinary recruit; but it was not until an
occasion when the Colonel and Officers gave a Ball that he
discovered his troop was harbouring a Scholar. Owing to
the outbreak of war the duration of the regiment's stay

at Reading was uncertain, and the Officers desired an opportunity of returning the hospitality which, since their arrival, they had received from the townsfolk and neighbouring gentry. A Ball was decided on, and selected N.C.O.'s and men were detailed for duty at the scene of the festivity—'Candlestick Duty', they termed it. The superior manners of Private Cumberback led to his being posted at the Ballroom door, where he stood all night in full-dress uniform—peaked helmet with red-and-white plume on the left side and horsehair crest from brow to back, a smart coatee with worsted epaulettes and pipeclayed shoulder-belt, a formidable sabre, skin-tight white breeches, and Hessian boots with spurs that clanked like fetters—a martial figure, indeed, little in accord with Wordsworth's later portrait of his friend as "the brooding Poet with the heavenly eyes".

And as rank and fashion whirled and fluttered before him, Captain Ogle and an Officer of another corps stopped near by for a moment just before joining the dancers. They were talking, oddly enough, of the classics and Greek poetry:—for in the eighteenth century educated men, even in the Army, would include such subjects in their conversation. The Officer misquoted a couple of lines in Greek, which he said were from Euripides. Coleridge could not pass this: the scholar in him rose above the sabreur, deep reading of the classics triumphed over discipline. "If your Honour will excuse me," he blurted out, "that's not quite accurate. They're from the *Œdipus* of Sophocles, and they run like this" . . . and he gave them correctly. "Why," asked the astonished Officer, "who the devil are you?" "The sentry, sir," answered Private Cumberback, "and your honour's servant!" The Officer stared a little, laughed, and then, shrugging his shoulders, strolled off to dance.

Captain Ogle said nothing, but was more than ever determined to solve this mystery. He took counsel with Surgeon Turner, the regimental Doctor, who, during his frequent treatments of Cumberback for sprains and bruises, had also discovered his superior intelligence and had determined to get him 'struck off' as hospital orderly as soon as the drill-sergeants and the riding-master had done with him. Turner, himself a dilettante of letters, had more than once had a mock-ferocious wrangle with his patient on points of prosody and verse-construction. But the two Officers knew each other and were equally interested in this strange recruit, who, they agreed, would be no loss to his Troop on parade. So that a compromise was arranged between them, whereby the lad should be 'struck off' as hospital orderly, but should each day be available at certain times for duty as his Troop-leader's servant.

IV

THE HOSPITAL-ORDERLY

For the Camp's stir and crowd and ceaseless 'larum,
The neighing warhorse, the ear-shattering trumpet,
The unvaried, still returning hour of duty,
Word of command and exercise of arms—
There's nothing here, there's nothing in all this.

THE change meant heaven for Coleridge: no guards, no
stables, no drill, and, above all, no riding-school. His
quarters were shifted to the hospital. Once he had wished
to be a Doctor like his elder brother Luke, who had been a
medical student in a London hospital while Coleridge was
at school; and on many a Saturday the little 'Blue' had
got leave to walk the wards with him, helping him with
dressings and bandages. He had read books on medicine
insatiably, and had devoured whole medical dictionaries.
A sufferer himself and frequently "in sense of pain", his
sympathy with other sufferers and his gift of companionship had now free play. In those days military hygiene in
the modern sense did not exist, and medicine and surgery
alike were almost primitive. Even in a single unit in
billets the normal sick list was heavy; and in the sick-bay,
medical and surgical casualties—slight and serious, con-
tagious cases and mere 'cuts and bruises'—were huddled

together: 'sore heads' and smallpox patients groaned side by side. Newspapers were scarce and expensive, and few of the men could read; but, through Surgeon Turner and Captain Ogle, Coleridge procured many books and read to the poor patients by the hour in the intervals of attending to their piteous wants. He became famous, too, as a story-teller; and the great wealth of his reading, adapted and abridged to the capacity of his listeners' understanding, was poured out for their benefit. The sagas of Homer and Virgil, Xenophon's retreat, the battles of Alexander, the feats of Froissart's chivalry, of Purchas's and Marco Polo's captains, the glory of Shakespeare and the fantasy of Spenser, held them enchanted. Long talks he gave them, too, in a colloquial idiom, on elementary Ethics and Philosophy—forerunners of those heavier monologues of his later days in Gillman's crowded sitting-room at High-gate. And the men soon declared that Silas with his talks did them more good than all the Doctor's stuff. Once, for six weeks, the gallant orderly, unhelped, looked after a smallpox case so virulent that even the Medical Officer agreed to its isolation. Alone with the patient in a stuffy outhouse, he tended him day and night, in delirium and in coma; and during convalescence he read to him un-tiringly.

The other part of Coleridge's new duties, as personal orderly to Captain Ogle, was equally congenial and still pleasanter in its incidence. The young Troop-leader was his senior in age: a man of good classical education.and with leanings towards literature, like so many then of his class and type. His reading was neither as wide nor deep as that of his bâtman, but he was an eager listener and controversialist when, in the seclusion of his quarters or on country rides and walks together, the two were able to talk on an equality. He was the only companion of the same class and intelligence whom Coleridge had encountered during his soldiering; and as their relations grew more intimate, the Captain soon extracted much of his true story from the Trooper and saw at once the folly of keeping so great a store of intellectual talents hidden beneath this bushel of barrack life. In spite of Coleridge's protestations and refusals to divulge the names of his relatives, Ogle set to work to make enquiries at Cambridge and so to get into touch with some authority or kinsman who could 'buy him out'.

About this time, too, Coleridge met by chance in the streets of Reading a newly commissioned Subaltern who had been his friend at Cambridge and who was then on his way to join his corps 'on first appointment'. With a smart salute the Trooper passed the Officer by, hoping that uniform would prove a sufficient disguise. But even a dragoon's peaked helmet did not avail to alter the deep grey eyes beneath it or the pink and white Devonshire skin of a face the Officer so well remembered having seen kindle in scholarly debate with mutual friends such as Butler or Bethell. (This was Christopher Bethell, of King's, the theologian: afterwards Bishop successively of Gloucester, Exeter and Bangor.) He called the fellow back and asked his name. "Private Cumberback, sir, Fifteenth

Light Dragoons", was the answer, given with hopeless unconvincingness. "That won't do: I know you", said the Subaltern not unsympathetically. "You're Coleridge, of Jesus, whom they've been looking for at Cambridge for the last six months. Don't go on with this foolery. I'm on my way to join my regiment, but I shall write them at once to say I've found you."

So the game was up at last for Trooper Silas. He recognized the inevitable and waited for it to happen, and carried on his duties meanwhile with mixed emotions. On the whole he had been happy as a soldier, and quite certainly he was physically fitter. The freedom from material cares, the healthy deadening level of daily routine, had purged him of dejection and ill-humours; and he had warmed to the rough kindly comradeship of men who had made a favourite of one with whom they had, excepting courage and a sense of humour, no single quality in common. But, with mental serenity and bodily health, somehow there had returned to him the Poet's urge for self-expression, the itch of authorship, the lust for literature and intellectual adventure. He saw the inkpots opening for him again; the paper spread. And in the readings to the men of the rare newspapers he had become aware of wider happenings in the world outside; of the great change developing in France, which, then in its early promise, had begun to fan the embers of his political philosophy. Already the seeds of 'Pantisocracy' were sowing themselves in his mind. The soldiering interlude had served its purpose and was drawing to a close. A little impatiently he would await its ending and prepare for the realization of his returned ambitions.

He had not long to wait. One morning, when he was busy in the hospital, the door was opened to admit Captain Ogle, the Adjutant, and Coleridge's eldest brother, James. Without a word they beckoned him; and without a word he left his work and followed them. The men who watched were now quite sure that he was a deserter. Before their hapless Cumberback they saw a Court-Martial looming, whose sentence of lashes would be carried out in hollow square of the regiment by a relentless Provost-Sergeant at the triangles. "Poor Silas", muttered someone (may it have been the smallpox convalescent?), "I hope they'll let him off with a cool five hundred!"

But James had come to buy his brother out.

V

BOOT AND SADDLE

Homeward I wend my way; and Lo! recalled
From bodings that have wellnigh wearied me,
I find myself upon the brow, and pause
Startled . . .

Cedant Arma Togae.

WHEN, in his shabby mufti once again, he passed the
sentry at gate to get into the chaise which was waiting to
take him back, the road before Coleridge seemed to
broaden and lengthen, almost terrifically. Somewhere, at
points along its wide perspective, were posted shapes,
vague immaterialities as yet—*Christabel, Alhadra, The
Ancient Mariner, Zapolya, Kubla Khan*—awaiting the touch
of his creative hand. Expectant, by every milestone, stood
some future friend—Southey and Wordsworth, the Wedg-
woods, Hazlitt and De Quincey. And, as he drove away,
listening to, though scarcely heeding, his brother's sour
reproaches, a trumpet blew 'Boot and Saddle'.

Long afterwards, in 'the silent sanctuary', perhaps, of
Stowey or in the hush of some summer night at Keswick,
there would return to him from the depths of long-buried
memories of his youth the faint re-echo of that trumpet-
call.

106

WALTER SCOTT

Quartermaster, ROYAL EDINBURGH LIGHT DRAGOONS
AND MIDLOTHIAN YEOMANRY

"Brown Adam" and The Quartermaster

TROOP-SONG

of

THE ROYAL EDINBURGH LIGHT DRAGOONS

To horse, to horse! the standard flies,
The bugles sound the call;
The Gallic navies stem the seas,
The voice of battle's on the breeze,
Arouse ye, one and all!

From high Dunedin's towers we come
A band of brothers true;
Our casques the leopard's spoils surround,
With Scotland's hardy thistle crown'd;
We boast the red and blue.

Though tamely crouch to Gallia's frown
Dull Holland's tardy train;
Their ravish'd toys though Romans mourn;
Though gallant Switzers vainly spurn,
And, foaming, gnaw the chain;

Oh! had they marked the avenging call
Their brethren's murder gave,
Disunion ne'er their ranks had mown
Nor patriot valour, desperate grown,
Sought freedom in the grave!

Shall we, too, bend the stubborn head
In Freedom's temple born,
Dress our pale cheek in timid smile
To hail a master in our isle
Or brook a victor's scorn?

AUTHORS-AT-ARMS

No! though destruction o'er the land
Comes pouring as a flood,
The sun that sees our falling day
Shall mark our sabres' deadly sway
And set that night in blood.

For gold let Gallia's legions fight,
Or plunder's bloody gain:
Unbribed, unbought, our swords we draw
To guard our King, to fence our law,
Nor shall their edge be vain.

If ever breath of British gale
Shall fan the tricolour,
Or footstep of invader rude,
With rapine foul and red with blood,
Pollute our happy shore,

Then farewell home, and farewell friends!
Adieu each tender tie!
Resolved we mingle in the tide
Where charging squadrons furious ride
To conquer or to die.

To horse! to horse! the sabres gleam,
High sounds the bugle call;
Combined by Honour's sacred tie
Our word is 'Laws and Liberty!'
March forward one and all!

I

SQUADRON-TRAINING AT MUSSELBURGH

Then here's a health to Wellington, to Beresford, to Long,
And a single word to Bonaparte before I close my song:
The eagles that to fight he brings
Should serve his men with wings
When they meet the bold dragoons with their long swords
  boldly riding:
Whack fal-de-ral, etc.

BEFORE the great door of a barn at Musselburgh, Midlothian—his improvised 'store'—the Quartermaster of the
Royal Edinburgh Light Dragoons, a regiment of volunteer
Light Cavalry which had marched into billets that day
from the Scottish capital for a fortnight's exercise, sat on
a truss of hay checking forage deliveries from the local
farmers. It is recorded that the weather was mild for the
time of year (March 1799), with a breeze blowing softly
down the Esk from southward; so that the Officer, a tall,
deep-chested young man of twenty-eight, had opened his
tight red jacket and loosened his stock beneath its stiff
collar of royal blue; though, to lend authority to his ruddy
genial face with its pug nose and humorous mouth, he
retained his imposing helmet. For ever since he had ridden
in some hours before with the advance-party, Quartermaster Scott had been hard at work arranging the head-

quarters-offices and the billets and messrooms previously bespoken, and checking ration-issues for distribution and purchase-invoices for fodder and litter brought in from the neighbouring countryside. His tongue was kept busy answering a thousand questions, and his pen—innocent as yet of any more noteworthy literary production than a verse-translation of Bürger's *Lenore*—had scribbled his signature to countless receipts and 'chits'. But he left his impromptu seat of office every other minute, hopping briskly here and there, cheerfully indefatigable in his arduous duties in spite of a marked lameness of his right leg, and keeping the dour Midlothian peasants in a good humour by waggish repartees in their own homely Doric.

For Quartermaster Scott had known the Esk country since boyhood and the previous year had taken a longish lease of a summer cottage at Lasswade, where his wife was now busy on her first layette, and where they had as neighbours some of his closest friends—the Clerks of Pennycuick, Mackenzie of Auchindenny ('The Man of Feeling'), Lord Woodhouselee, and the great families of Dundas and Buccleuch. As soon as the trumpeter's dinner-call announced that his morning's work was over, the Quartermaster buttoned up his jacket and limped off to join a group of brother Officers before the messroom, outside which they walked up and down, chatting and laughing and recounting the morning's adventures until the mess-corporal should announce that the meal was ready. It was on a similar occasion later in the training that Scott had as a mess-guest Matt Lewis—then travelling in the North in search of materials for his *Tales of Wonder*—who had been introduced to him by Walter Erskine and whose macabre book *The Monk*, with its interpolation of romantic ballads, had rekindled his poetic ambition. Outside the messroom, Cornet Skene, an enthusiast for German *volkslieder* since his school-days in Saxony, recited the German *kriegslied* 'Der Abschieds Tag ist da!' to the waiting group, much to Lewis's delight, and with such effect on the Quartermaster that next morning he produced 'The War-song of the Edinburgh Light Dragoons', a dashing battle-piece in the same metre. After mess that night, Scott was made to read this; and did so with so much spirit that it was forthwith adopted as the regimental troop-song.

The experiment of that March was the R.E.L.D.'s first experience of field training; for an Act of Parliament of the previous year had authorized all Volunteer Corps to go into billets for continuous instruction for any period not exceeding twenty days. And, though it had been raised two years before in 1797, the regiment had hitherto had to rely for its efficiency on drills in Edinburgh parks or on the sands at Leith. Its C.O., Major Charles Maitland of Rankeillor, was an ex-regular Officer of some twenty years' service; and Lieutenant John Adams, its Adjutant, with Cunningham the regimental Sergeant-Major, had been transferred to the new corps from the Royal Cinque Ports Light Dragoons, an English Yeomanry regiment which had been for some time in garrison at Edinburgh. But Quartermaster Scott, then a junior member of the Faculty of Advocates, had had no experience of the sort, and was now working out in practice arrangements the elaboration of which on paper had kept him burning the midnight oil for weeks beforehand. A natural zest, however, for detailed and onerous paper-work, a determination to make the first Training a success from the 'Q' side, and an innate brisk-ness of mind and body, enabled him to cope with duties that involved a complete abandonment for the time being of his civilian interests, professional and intellectual. "I think I could give you some more crumbs of information were I at home," he wrote to a fellow-student of romantic literature, "but I am at present discharging the duties of Quartermaster to a regiment of Volunteer Light Cavalry —an office altogether inconsistent with romance; for where do you read that Sir Tristrem weighed out hay and corn, that Sir Lancelot du Lac distributed billets, or that any knight of the Round Table condescended to higgle about a truss of straw?" There were complications, too, in the subsistence expenses of both mounts and men; for the price of forage was high and Scott was hard put to it to make both ends meet for his horses on the Government allowance; while the gentlemen troopers were apt to do themselves too well. And when it was discovered that the expense of messing, even allowing for the deduction of the Government's 3s. 4d. per day for rations, exceeded 5s., the Regimental Committee recommended at his instance that "the Duty-Officer of the day or his Orderly-Sergeant should overlook the distribution of wine and prevent the jocular devices by which the vigilance of mess-waiters was so often over-reached".

But on the Rhine, but on the Rhine they cluster,
The grapes of juice divine that make our troopers' courage
    muster:
Oh, blessed be the Rhine!

The billeting, also, of the numerous private servants and
grooms of the gentlemen troopers was a difficulty, though
each one's expenses were provided by his master. Scott
himself had no groom, but as a good horsemaster took a
pride in feeding his own charger first thing in the morning,
and "combing the mane of his courser bold like Edda when
Lôk paid him a visit"—a practice that he continued even
down to Abbotsford days. He had written to his uncle at
Kelso to look out for "a strong gelding such as would suit
a stalwart Dragoon" and, with regard to price, that he
would sell his prized collection of Scottish coins "sooner
than not be mounted to his mind".

The fortnight's training at Musselburgh was, both
militarily and socially, a complete success; and when it
terminated on March 25 after an Inspection of the regiment by the General Officer Commanding the Forces in
Scotland, a dinner was given by the Magistrates to the
troops in compliment to the regular and orderly conduct
of the corps while quartered there, during which each
Officer and man was made a freeman of the town. On the
return to Edinburgh the Regimental Committee, reviewing
the lessons of the exercise on the administrative side, was
evidently of opinion that the Quartermaster had been
overworked. For, while paying due tribute to his zeal and
capacity, it recommended that he should in future have

the assistance of two N.C.O.'s or troopers who should be responsible under his orders for the issue of all corn, hay, and straw; and in consideration of the fact that he was already Secretary of the Committee, that he should be relieved of the duties of Paymaster which he had hitherto carried out by the appointment to that post of Cornet Colin Mackenzie of Portmore (later to be a brother Clerk of Session with him). A tribute and recommendation which must certainly have gratified the Quartermaster's young wife in her pretty new house in North Castle Street, as she glanced proudly at the miniature (a present from him on their wedding-day some fifteen months before) which hung above the drawing-room mantelpiece and represented the efficient young Officer in all the glory of his full-dress uniform.

They had met in the summer of 1797 when Scott was spending the vacation with his brother John, then a Captain in the 73rd, and Adam Fergusson of the Edinburgh Infantry Volunteers (and later of the 58th Foot), on a riding tour across the Border in Northumberland. Near Gilsland one morning they chanced to pass a girl on horseback whose looks and horsemanship all three admired. She was, they soon discovered, staying in the same house: and at a County Ball that evening which John and Adam attended in full regimentals, though she danced frequently with both resplendent warriors, it was Walter in his civilian livery of sober black (for the Light Dragoons had not yet been issued with their uniforms) who took her down to a prolonged and ecstatic supper, from which both rose irrevocably in love. Charlotte Charpentier was the daughter of a French *émigrée* widow from Lyons, and the ward of Lord Downshire, an old friend and patron of her parents. A *petite brunette* with large eyes of an expressive brown, she spoke with an entrancing French accent, was gay and intelligent, and had £500 a year of her own. Under the chaperonage of her old governess, Miss Nicholson, granddaughter of the Dean of Carlisle, she was on her way to stay indefinitely at the latter's Deanery to escape the attentions in London of some attractive detrimental, whose memory in the lady's heart and mind quickly began to melt before the ardour of the limping Light Dragoon. Within a week or two they were engaged; and when Scott returned to his Courts for the beginning of term from a halcyon visit to the Deanery, an impassioned correspondence ensued; in the course of which Scott discussed plans for the future, including at one time the idea of emigration to the Colonies. But Mademoiselle Charlotte had been through a London Season and was attracted by the prospect of life in the Scottish capital, where she regarded his prospects, professional and social, as sufficiently promising. For she had come to realize that he was there an accepted and acceptable member of an influential circle of select and clever people, and she had no hankering for the hardships of a backwoods life. "I am glad," she confessed quite naïvely in one delicious letter, "that you don't give up the *Cavalry*, as I love something that is *stylish*. With all my love and those sort of pretty things— Charlotte."

They exchanged miniatures—the Light Dragoons' uniform was sanctioned just in time to set the colour-scheme of his in blue and scarlet. Scott toasted her twenty times or so at a bachelor dinner to his brother Officers and friends that lasted till one in the morning. And on Christmas Eve at St. Mary's Church, Carlisle, Mademoiselle Charlotte became the Quartermaster's wife.

II

THE GENTLEMEN MOSS-TROOPERS

Sound, sound the clarion, fill the fife!

THERE is little doubt that it was to the zeal of Walter Scott himself that the regiment of Edinburgh Light Dragoons owed its origin. He confessed that, but for a permanent lameness of his right leg which had resulted from infantile paralysis, he would have been a soldier. Though his father was a peace-loving Writer-to-the-Signet with an austere presbyterian mistrust of all things military, his old kinsman Sir George MacDougal of Mackerstoun, an ex-Colonel of the Greys, had made a favourite of Walter as a child; at Prestonpans a veteran of the German wars, Captain Dalgetty (a name he was to make immortal), and in the Highlands old Stewart of Invernahyle, a Jacobite campaigner who had been 'out in the '45', had filled his boyhood's dreams with soldierly ambitions. His second brother, John, was an Officer in the 73rd (now the 2nd Battalion, The Black Watch); and when after the Convention's declaration of war against England in 1793, volunteer regiments sprang into being throughout the United Kingdom and his younger brother Tom joined the new Edinburgh Infantry Volunteers and afterwards the 70th Foot (The East Surrey Regiment) as Paymaster, Walter grew jealously restless and sick at heart. His lameness precluded infantry service either in the Militia or Volunteers: he was a good horseman and loved horses, but as an impecunious young barrister of only two years' standing, living as a dependent at his father's house in a city square, he had no hope of admission to the Yeomanry, as the Volunteer Cavalry then began to be called. For the Yeomanry regiments were strictly territorial and rural in composition, consisting of troops of tenantry and 'bonnet lairds' who owned their own horses, officered by gentlemen of the county aristocracy. Three years later, however, the menace of a French invasion became still more acute, and the news of the formation in London of Light Horse Volunteer regiments recruited from among young business and professional men in Westminster and the City, inspired Scott to propose to his University and legal friends the formation of a similar corps in Edinburgh. The idea 'caught on'. A meeting attended by youths at the University and young advocates, solicitors, and commercial men was held at the Royal Exchange Coffee-house on February 14, 1797, and an offer of the services of all present as Light Cavalry, without pay, and mounted and armed by themselves or with such arms as the Government might provide, was forwarded to the War Office. And an intimation was published in the newspapers that further applications to join should be sent to Mr. Walter Scott, Advocate, George Square, who had been appointed Secretary of the Committee. This was followed in March by a further meeting to settle details, and in April the War Office intimated His Majesty's approval of the formation of a Volunteer Light Cavalry Regiment of two troops to be called 'The Royal Edinburgh Light Dragoons'. The uniform prescribed, of a typical eighteenth-century extravagance, consisted of a dragoon helmet of black leather with a semicircular crest of leopard's skin, garnished on the left by a red-and-white hackle and on the right by a thistle badge; a scarlet shell-jacket with silver shoulder-ridges and collar and facings of blue and silver; close white leather breeches and black jack-boots and spurs. (The French Revolutionary armies acquired for their Chasseurs-à-Cheval the Magyar dress and the designation 'Hussars' from the Hungarian Irregular Horse employed by their Austrian enemies; and it was not until later on in the Napoleonic wars that the title and uniform were in turn adopted for Light Cavalry by their opponents of the British Army.) The name of the Major-Commandant was left over until November—when Major Maitland was appointed; but the other Officers were selected by ballot among the members of the corps, for confirmation in their commissions by the Lord-Lieutenant; and the N.C.O.'s with their respective seniority were similarly chosen. William Rae of St. Catherine's (afterwards Lord-Advocate) was nominated Captain; William Forbes of Pitsligo and James Skene of Rubislaw were the two Cornets; and Walter Scott was appointed Paymaster, Quartermaster, and Secretary of the Regimental Committee. The Farrier was Alexander Gray, who declined any extra emolument for his responsible duties, declaring himself amply satisfied with the honour of serving in the corps. By June 16 the two troops were fully constituted, and, with the Infantry Volunteers, were inspected at Bruntsfield by General Sir James Stewart, G.O.C. at Edinburgh. At the conclusion of the inspection, a regimental standard, worked by herself and other ladies, was presented by Miss Paton of Kinaldy. These 'Gentlemen Moss-troopers' of the Edinburgh Light Dragoons were all young men of professional or social standing—youthful lairds and aristocrats, University graduates and students, Advocates, Writers-to-the-Signet, and merchants. The corps was, in fact, what would now be termed in the Territorial Army or Senior O.T.C. a 'Class-Corps'—analogous to the Cavalry Squadron in the Universities' O.T.C.'s and 'The Devil's Own', or to the Horse Batteries of the H.A.C.

Daily drills, mounted and dismounted, were at once started in a park near the Botanic Garden and on Leith Sands; and both troops paraded daily for these at 5 A.M. As no member of the corps had any soldiering experience, instructors were borrowed from among the N.C.O.'s of the Cinque Ports Dragoons, then in garrison; and twice a week Staff-Sergeant Cunningham of that regiment took the Officers at sword exercise. Though his duties were mainly administrative, and had been selected for him according to Cornet Skene "so as to spare him the rough usage of the ranks", Scott, as a good horseman with a passionate desire to prove that his leg disability was negligible in the saddle, insisted on parading with his troop. "His zeal and animation", wrote Skene, "served to sustain the enthusiasm of the whole corps, while his ready *mot-à-rire* kept up in all a degree of good-humour and relish for the service without which the toil and privation of long daily drills would not easily have been submitted to by such a body of gentlemen. At every interval of exercise the order 'Sit at ease' was the signal for the Quartermaster to lead the squadron to merriment: every eye was intuitively turned on 'Earl Walter', as he was familiarly called by his associates of that date, and his ready joke seldom failed to raise the ready laugh. He took his full share, too, in all the labours and duties of the corps; had the highest pride in its progress and proficiency, and was such a trooper himself as only a very powerful frame of body and the warmest zeal in the cause could have enabled anyone to be." Lord Cockburn, in his *Memorials*, notes the same keenness: "He was the soul of the Edinburgh troop. It was not a duty with him, nor a necessity, but an absolute passion, indulgence in which gratified his feudal taste for war and his jovial socialness. He drilled and drank and made songs with a hearty conscientious earnestness which inspired or shamed everybody within the attraction. I do not know if it is usual, but his troop used to practise individually with a sabre at a turnip, which was stuck on the top of a staff to represent a Frenchman in front of the line. Every other trooper, when he set forward in his turn, was far less concerned about the success of his aim than about how he was to tumble. But Walter frisked forward gallantly, saying to himself 'Cut them down, the villains! Cut them down!'

and cordially made his blow—which from his lameness was often an awkward one—muttering curses all the while at the detested enemy." (If the horse be eliminated, this seems almost a prophetic picture of a recruit at practice on a bayonet-course during a similar national emergency one hundred and seventeen years later.) It was written of him in that first year: "Not an idea crosses his mind or a word his lips that has not an allusion to some damned instrument or evolution of the cavalry—'Draw your swords!,—By single files to the right of the front!,—To the left, wheel!;—Charge!' " And *à propos* of charging and Scott's reputation as the comedian of the corps, Trooper Guthrie Wright, then Auditor (or Taxing-Master) of the Court of Session, wrote to Lockhart: "My rear-rank man rode a great brute of a carriage-horse over which he had not sufficient control, and which, therefore, not infrequently broke at a charge through the front rank, and he could not pull him up till he had got several yards ahead of the troop. One day, as we were standing at ease after this occurred, I was rather grumbling, I suppose, at one of my legs being carried off in this unceremonious way; when Scott said, 'Why, sir, I think you are most properly placed in your present position, as you know it is your special business to check *over-charges!*" (Their familiar use of a nickname or some endearing *soubriquet* is no bad criterion of a man's popularity with his fellows. Here are a few which flew round the fireplace in the Parliament House or round the messroom the instant Scott appeared: 'Wattie', the earliest and most widely used; 'Earl Walter' and 'Duke of

Darnick' from his leanings to aristocratic chivalry; 'Colonel Grogg', from a conspicuous pair of grogram breeches; 'Duns' or 'Duns Scotus', from his antiquarian propensities; and, in later years, 'The Shirra' to all and sundry, from his Shrieval office.)

In the peculiar circumstances of the time and owing to the class-character of the self-recruited regiment, the original committee which had initiated its formation was allowed to continue administrative functions after that event had been officially sanctioned. Indeed, the authorities of a War Department which had not yet been organized with a view to expansion in time of national emergency were only too pleased to leave questions of interior economy, and even of discipline, in a volunteer corps to its constituent members so long as its military obligations and efficiency were maintained. So that the interior administration of the Edinburgh Light Dragoons, in common with those of many such citizen formations at that period, was conducted very much on the lines of a club. The Committee of Management consisted of the Officers (including the C.O., who might almost be said in this regard to have been only *primus inter pares*) and one representative elected by each troop. It met weekly, or more often as necessity demanded, to transact the financial and administrative business of the corps; in matters of doubt or difficulty referring the case for consideration to a general meeting of all the members. It dealt with the acceptance or rejection of candidates for enrolment, and drafted Standing Orders for general approval, together with the amount of fines exactable for non-observance. On some points the Committee, as in other Fencible corps, communicated direct with the Secretary for War—almost in the manner of a Spanish military Junta, though there is no recorded case of any attempt to exercise political pressure. But direct representations were made from Edinburgh on such questions, for instance, as permanent pay for a sergeant and trumpeter per troop, the issue of arms and equipment to replace those originally found by the men themselves, and pay and horse-allowances during trainings. The Committee also arranged for training-areas, and on one occasion when the tide was inconvenient at Leith applied to the Magistrates to be allowed to ride over the Links at Bruntsfield. To this, however, the Society of Golfers raised strong objection; and the Bench, 'out of respect for that ancient and useful body' and in spite of the fact that French warships were reconnoitring the British coastline and emergency measures were being arranged for the removal of the Court, if necessary, to Worcester, refused permission — an incident strangely prototypical of similar instances of unpatriotic imbecility in 1914–15. The Committee's disciplinary powers did not extend to orders actually given on parade or during operations, but they governed cases of unpunctuality or non-attendance, for which it was intimated that neither 'the amusement of hunting' nor business engagements would be accepted as excuses. After the weekly meetings, which were held in the Officers' houses in rotation, the members of the Committee and their wives and friends dined or supped as the guests of the Officer

whose house had been the meeting-place; and these enter-
tainments became a recognized feature of social life in
Edinburgh for many years, long after the menace of
French invasion had disappeared. On such occasions the
Quartermaster was at his best. A brilliant conversation-
alist with an inexhaustible fund of anecdote and allusion,
he loved conviviality and excelled in chaffing repartee. His
wit was not so much what his compatriots describe as
'pawky' as an overflowing exuberance of high spirits which
compelled a similar humour and enjoyment in others. He
possessed the social gift to a supreme degree. Recalling
these evenings, he wrote in 1808:

> Eleven years we now may tell,
> Since we have known each other well:
> Since, riding side by side, our hand
> First drew the voluntary brand.
>
> *   *   *   *   *
>
> In merry chorus well combined
> With laughter drowned the whistling wind.
> Mirth was within, and Care without
> Might gnaw her nails to hear our shout.

Mrs. Scott, who adored society, good talk, and pretty
clothes, had from the first been a success in Edinburgh,
and made close friends among the wives of her husband's
brother Officers—among whom Mrs. William Forbes of
Pitsligo had been his first love. The daughter of Sir
William Belches of Invermay and Lady Jane Stuart, a
school friend of Walter's mother, she was the 'Greenmantle' of *Redgauntlet*. They had been child friends; and

when he met her later, grown-up and 'out', the young and penniless law student was so imprudent as to make most sheepish and devoted love to her. She liked him well enough; but when, at twenty-four, he wrote her a proposal of marriage she sent him a non-committal reply telling him to wait a while. The poor youth took it as an acceptance, and when in the same year she got engaged to his brother Officer, William Forbes of Pitsligo, a baronet-banker's son whom she married two years later, his spirit was crushed—at any rate until he met his Charlotte six months afterwards. The two couples, however, were constantly in each other's company at the Light Dragoon dinners, at which Cornet Skene also brought his wife, who was Forbes's sister. Poor 'Greenmantle'! She died in 1810 when the whole country was ringing with *The Lady of the Lake*; while Charlotte lived on to be a baronet's wife at Abbotsford.

III

THE RIGHT SQUADRON

For, like Mad Tom's, our chiefest care
Was horse to ride and sword to wear.

AFTER the passing of the Volunteer Act in 1798 the
Government issued an appeal for recruits, and the response in Edinburgh and the neighbourhood sufficed to
fill the gaps in the files of the Light Dragoons, caused by
the transfer of troopers to the commissioned ranks of the
Militia and of other mounted units, in plenty of time for
the King's Birthday Parade of the garrison and volunteers
in June and the annual Yeomanry Inspection in the following month. In the succeeding March came the first
billeting of the regiment at Musselburgh before referred
to; but, during the autumn and winter, vacancies multi-
plied in this eighteenth-century O.T.C. and the regiment
was again under strength owing to commissions accepted
by members in other corps and the Regular Army. A
scheme for amalgamation with the Midlothian Yeomanry
was therefore put on foot, and early in 1800 was authorized
by the War Office. The two original troops of the Light
Dragoons retained their identity and personnel, but became the Right Squadron of the reconstituted regiment,

the Left Squadron being composed of four Midlothian Yeomanry troops from Hermiston, Dalkeith, Cramond, and Dalmahoy respectively: and Lieutenant-Colonel Trotter of the Midlothians, as senior Field Officer, took over command of the whole. Before the annual exercise at Musselburgh—a practice of the Light Dragoons which was continued by the new Yeomanry unit—the corps was called out to assist the Magistrates in suppressing the famous 'Meal Riots'. The disturbances continued for a week, at the conclusion of which the regiment received the thanks of the Lord Provost and the Home Secretary for its services. In 1801 a similar emergency occurred, and it must have been at this period of duty 'in assistance of the Civil Power' that there occurred 'the Affair of Moredun Mill', the mention of which by Scott fourteen years later so mystified the Czar Alexander I. Half a troop, under Cornets Skene and Spottiswoode and the Quartermaster, dispersed a force of rioters which had assembled to loot the mill at Moredun. The male rioters took refuge in the neighbouring coal-pits, leaving the women to be dislodged from a large building to which a dismounted party under Scott eventually gained access. Scott bundled the most violent of these women-at-arms into a farm-cart, which was driven off in charge of Spottiswoode amid the cheers of Yeomen and amazons alike; and the *émeute* ended in good humour, brought about largely by the Quartermaster's tactful handling of the situation.

* * * * *

In consequence of the large-scale preparations for the

invasion of England made in 1803 by Napoleon after the
short-lived peace of Amiens, the regiment was on permanent duty practically throughout that year; in billets at
Dalkeith, Musselburgh, and at Lasswade—conveniently
close to the Quartermaster's summer cottage. Inspections
were frequent: the most important being by Lord Moira,
the new Commander-in-Chief, on Portobello Sands in
October; and it was at this period during a charge on the
Sands that Scott received a kick from a horse which laid
him up in his quarters for three days. In this short time he
began and finished Canto I of *The Lay of the Last Minstrel*,
"a kind of Romance of Border chivalry in a 'light-
horseman' sort of stanza". He wrote to a correspondent in
July: "We are assuming a very military appearance. Three
regiments of Militia, with a formidable park of Artillery,
are encamped just by us. Our Edinburgh Troop, of which
I have the honour to be Quartermaster, consists entirely of
young gentlemen of family, and is, of course, admirably
well mounted and armed. There are four other troops in
the regiment, consisting of Yeomanry, whose iron faces
and muscular forms announce the hardness of the climate
against which they wrestle and the powers which Nature
has given them to contend with and subdue it. These
corps have been easily raised in Scotland, the farmers
being, in general, a high-spirited race of men, fond of
active exercise and patient in hardship and fatigue. For
myself, I must own that to one who, like myself, has
la tête un peu exaltée, 'the pomp and circumstance of war'
give for a time a very poignant and pleasing sensation. The

imposing appearance of cavalry, in particular, and the rush which makes their onset appear to me to partake highly of the sublime. Perhaps I am more attached to this sort of sport of swords because my health requires much active exercise, and a lameness contracted in childhood renders it inconvenient for me to take it otherwise than on horse-back."

In October the system of signal-beacons to spread the alarm on the sighting of the invaders had been completed —one of them, to connect with that on Edinburgh Castle, having been placed in front of Scott's cottage at Lasswade. The country felt that Buonaparte meant business this time. By day and night men's eyes were anxiously turned seaward.

False alarms were not infrequent. On the night of January 31, 1804, the N.C.O. in charge of the beacon on Hume Castle mistook a charcoal-burner's fire across the Border in Northumberland for the southward signal, and lit his own. What followed resembles the description in Macaulay's *Armada* of a similar happening in the past. The hills on both sides the Border, in Roxburgh, Selkirk, and the Lothians, became volcanoes from Kelso to Dalkeith; though on the coast the warning got no farther than St. Abb's Head. Militia proceeded to their war-stations by forced marches, and Yeomen and Volunteers hastened to their alarm-posts. At the time, the Scotts were at Gilsland in Northumberland, the place of their first romantic meeting seven years before: she had driven there at leisure from Edinburgh with her husband riding beside the carriage. When the news came, the Quartermaster saddled his horse and, crossing the Cheviots and the intervening shires, in twenty-four hours had covered the odd hundred miles between Gilsland and Dalkeith, his regimental rendezvous. Here he found his own corps, together with the Selkirkshire Yeomanry and several units of local Infantry Volunteers; and advantage was taken by the G.O.C. to exercise the troops in a few days' combined training, before, the alarm having been confirmed as false, the units dispersed again and Scott rode southward to rejoin his wife.

Scott used the incident as the *dénouement* of *The Antiquary* in which he made 'Old Caxon' the delinquent, and pictured Mr. Oldbuck, armed with the sword his father wore in 'the '45', watching the 'Glenallan Yeomanry' march into 'Fairport'. In a note, while refraining from mention of his own experience, he pays tribute, as a brother Yeoman and the Sheriff of their county, to the performance of the Selkirkshire Yeomanry; "who made a remarkable march; for although some of the individuals lived at 20 or 30 miles distance from the place of muster, they were nevertheless embodied and in order in so short a period that they were at Dalkeith, their alarm-post, about one o'clock on the day succeeding the first signal, with men and horses in good order though the roads were in a bad state and many of the troopers must have ridden 40 or 50 miles without drawing bridle." He mentions, too, the presence of mind of the bride of one and the widowed mother of another of the Selkirkshires who happened to be away at the time in Edinburgh: these 'Roman matrons'—one young, one old —immediately dispatched thither the arms, uniforms, and chargers of the two troopers, that they might join their regiment at Dalkeith. "For", explained the older lady to Scott, "none can know better than you that my son is the only prop by which, since his father's death, our family is supported. But I would rather see him dead on that hearth than hear that he had been a horse's length behind his comrades in defence of his King and Country." (*A propos* the Selkirkshires, Willie Laidlaw, the 'factor' at Abbotsford, and a Selkirkshire Yeoman, professed contempt for James Ballantyne—Scott's printer, who had formerly been a tailor—because he had once measured the Yeomanry in Selkirk for new breeches.) But the tension continued during 1804-5, and troops throughout the country underwent an intensive and semi-continuous system of instruction which embraced much combined field training of the three arms. It was, indeed, because of a mild protest by the Lord-Lieutenant of Selkirkshire (of which county Scott was now Sheriff-Depute) about military duty sometimes interfering with the prompt administration of justice, that the Sheriff-Quartermaster took a lease of his cousin's house at Ashestiel in order to have a local habitation within his area of jurisdiction. In March the Midlothians took part with infantry and artillery in a scheme of attack and defence on Leith Links, and had occasion to charge the obstinate squares of a regiment of Highland Fencibles supported by Field Artillery, in prophetic anticipation of Waterloo—with the vital difference that the scheme involved the annihilation of the infantry. But the dour Highlanders cared nothing for 'Special Ideas'; and no orders of their Officers could induce them to give way before contemptible Lowland 'pock-puddings'. Colonel Murray MacGregor, their C.O., pictured himself being reprimanded by Lord Moira, the G.O.C., for inability to handle his battalion in accordance with instructions, and in despair galloped up to his supporting gunners shouting "Open the field-pieces on 'em!" For, as he tried to explain to the General's Staff-Officer, nothing less than grapeshot would induce his Highlanders to yield their ground. On his galloper's report Lord Moira instantly changed the scheme, which thus became, much to the disgust of the Yeomanry, an actual presage of Waterloo. Captain Jack Adams, the fat and jovial Kentish Yeomanry Officer who had been posted as Adjutant to the Light Dragoons seven years before, died while with the regiment at Musselburgh this year. As Quartermaster and Adjutant, Scott and he had worked together with one mind; for Adams was a good soldier, a great favourite, and a hearty boon-companion towards whom Scott's heart warmed. He was buried with military honours in Greyfriars Churchyard, where the regiment paraded with the G.O.C. and Staff and an Officers' party of the 1st Royal Edinburghs. It was at the suggestion of the Quartermaster, who remembered his jovial friend's dislike of all such gloomy ceremonial, that the band played the troops home to the tune of a popular and, perhaps, not inappropriate, ditty, "I hae laid a Herrin' in Saut". After Trafalgar, the threat of a French invasion disappeared, and in common with other Yeomanry regiments the Midlothians ceased intensive training. In

October of 1807, however, they joined the Peebleshire Yeomanry for field exercises at Musselburgh, and it was then that Scott, who had already begun work on *Marmion*, roughed-out the cantos describing Flodden. "In the intervals of drilling", noted the invaluable Skene—now a troopleader,—"he used to delight in walking his powerful black steed up and down upon the Portobello Sands within the beating of the surge; and now and then you would see him plunge in his spurs and go off, as it were, at the charge, with the spray dashing about him. As we rode back to Musselburgh he often came and placed himself beside me at the head of the troop to repeat the verses that he had been composing during these pauses of our exercise." Though thirty-six, the Sheriff-Deputy of Selkirkshire, a Clerk of Session, and by now a man of literary eminence, the Quartermaster was still the chartered comedian at any rate of the two Edinburgh troops. On an occasion during a 'stand-easy', when the men had dismounted and were slackening girths, some joke of Scott's raised so loud and sudden a laugh among those round him that it stampeded the horses, which galloped away over the Sands upsetting the horse-holders and kicking and biting each other as the saddles worked loose; some, indeed, took to the sea and swam in the direction of the Fifeshire coast. Most of them returned at the trumpet-call, but the swimmers only came back after the trumpeters had gone in after them stirrup-deep.

* * * * *

And so, though the incentive which originated it had

been removed, through all the years that followed down to 1814 Walter Scott retained his commission and duties as a Quartermaster of Yeomanry, in spite of his position as a Poet acclaimed, a Friend of Royalty, the Laird of Abbotsford since 1811, and (incognito) the author of *Waverley*. (As to this last, David Hume, nephew of the historian, was then of opinion that the unknown author "must be of a Jacobite family and predilections, a *Yeomanry Cavalryman*, and a Scottish Lawyer".)

IV

THE QUARTERMASTER'S CHARGERS

Not but amid the buxom scene
Some grave discourse might intervene
Of the good horse that bore him best,
His shoulders, hoof, and arching crest . . .

SCOTT was one of those favoured beings with whom horses
'go kindly'. The misfortune of his lameness had intensified
his devotion to and understanding of horseflesh; for since
childhood he had ridden when others walked. Though a
heavyweight all his life, with the riding-muscles of his
right leg atrophied, his fine balance and exceptional hands
ensured a good seat and control. As a youth he rode about
the Liddesdale country with his uncle Robert on a pony
called *Earwig*, his favourite for many years, on which in
1796 he had ridden to Invermay to court 'Greenmantle'
and from whose back he saw his Charlotte for the first
time. His earliest charger was a big bay animal which he
christened *Lenore* after his first published poem, and which
served him on parade until in 1803 he bought *Lieutenant*,
'a powerful black', according to Skene, which he rode
regularly both as a charger and during his earlier days as
Sheriff at Ashestiel. Later he purchased another black
called *Captain*, which he rode in the ranks for years, and on

which, during the hurricane and flood of August 1807, he
swam the swollen ford across the Tweed. "The ford was
never a good one, and for some time it remained not a
little perilous. Scott was the first to attempt its passage on
his favourite black horse *Captain*, who had scarcely entered
the river when he plunged beyond his depth and had to
swim to the other side. It requires a good horseman to
swim a deep and rapid stream, but Scott trusted to the
vigour of his sturdy trooper, and in spite of his lameness
kept his seat manfully." His next charger was a successful
experiment in another colour, for *Brown Adam* (so named
after one of the heroes of *Border Minstrelsy*) was intractable
in any other hands and would only be fed and ridden by
his master. Scott would saddle and bridle *Brown Adam* in
his stall and then open the door, when the horse would
at once trot out to beside the mounting-stone, where he
stood motionless until the Quartermaster was comfortably settled in the saddle; "after which he displayed his joy
by neighing triumphantly through a brilliant succession
of curvettings". Yet this horse was so great a rogue with
others that he broke the arm of one groom and the leg of
another.

(It was during the *Brown Adam* period that James Hogg,
the Ettrick Shepherd-Poet, importuned Scott to use his
influence with Lord Dalkeith to obtain for him a commission in the Militia. The Yeomanry Quartermaster,
however, pointed out that the pay was small for one without private means, and—as delicately as possible—that a
man in Hogg's station might find his relations with his

brother Officers a little unsatisfactory. Hogg was constrained to admit that he might not be possessed, perhaps, of either the psychological or social essentials for commissioned rank, but asserted stoutly that he would enlist in a marching regiment. Sheep, however, prevailed ultimately over soldiering in the Shepherd-Poet's ambitions, for he accepted instead a little farm rent-free from the Duke of Buccleuch.)

Brown Adam's good qualities and points would seem to have shaken Scott's enthusiasm for blacks, for his next—and last—charger was *Daisy*, a speckless white hunter, "high-spirited and very handsome, with such a mane as Rubens loved to paint". He, like *Brown Adam*, commended himself to the Quartermaster by standing like a rock for that pathetic lifting across the saddle of the crippled leg. But it was *Daisy* who, in his own fashion, first intimated to his master, then in his forty-fifth year, that the time had come to retire from active horse-soldiering. It was on the occasion of Scott's return to Abbotsford after attending the Allies' fêtes in Paris in 1815. "When he was brought to the door," Scott told his son-in-law, "instead of signifying by the usual tokens that he was pleased to see his master, he looked askant at me like the devil; and when I put my foot in the stirrup he reared bolt upright, and I fell to the ground rather awkwardly. The experiment was repeated twice or thrice, always with the same result. It occurred to me that he might have taken some capricious dislike to my dress, and Tom Purdie (the factotum at Abbotsford)—who always falls heir to the white hat and green jacket and so forth when Mrs. Scott has made me discard a set of garments—was sent for to try whether these habiliments would produce a similar reception from his old friend; but *Daisy* allowed Tom to back him with all manner of gentleness. The thing was inexplicable. But he had certainly taken some part of my conduct in high dudgeon and disgust, and after trying him again after the interval of a week, I was obliged to part with *Daisy*—and, wars and rumours of wars being over, I resolved thenceforth to have done with such dainty blood. I now stick to a good sober cob." (The sober cob was a little mare named *Sybil Grey*, on which, or on her successor, the 'Shirra' used to jog to such of his Courts as were held within convenient riding distance; when he would always pull up on the hill above Bemersyde to gaze on the aspect thence of his beloved landscape. And at this same spot on that golden September day in 1832, when his body was on its way to its final resting-place at Dryburgh, his horse, whichever it was—now harnessed in team to the hearse—insisted on stopping as usual, as though to sense the memory of his touch on the reins at the accustomed place and for the last time to share that moment with him. Skene did a watercolour sketch of Dryburgh in its valley at the request of Scott during an earlier illness, when, in agony from gallstones, he had expressed a wish to "see the place where I would lie", and where, in fact, he now sleeps, not far from another great Lowland laird and a still more famous cavalry-man, Earl Haig of Bemersyde.)

The idiosyncrasies of his horses formed a favourite

problem to Scott. "These creatures", he wrote to a friend, "have many thoughts of their own, no doubt, that we can never penetrate. Maybe some bird had whispered to *Daisy* that I had been to see the grand reviews at Paris on a little scrag of a Cossack, while my own gallant trooper was left at home bearing Peter and the postbag into Melrose." The allusion is to his having met Count Platoff, a Hetman of Cossacks under the Czar Alexander I, at a grand State dinner given in Paris by Lord Cathcart—once Commander-in-Chief in Scotland but then British Ambassador to the Czar: when Platoff had taken a great fancy to him and pressed him warmly to join his Staff at the next review, promising to mount him on one of the quietest of his Ukraine ponies. At the dinner, Scott, who attended in full uniform, was introduced by their host to the Czar. Noticing his lameness, the Emperor asked him, "In what affair were you wounded?" and the explanation came that the infirmity was a natural one. On which the Czar said, "I thought Lord Cathcart mentioned that you had served?" And the Quartermaster replied: "Yes, in a sense I served—at home in the Yeomanry Cavalry, a force resembling the Landwehr or Landsturm". "Under what Commander?" was the Czar's next query; and Scott gave the name of his troop-leader—"Under the Chevalier Rae". "Were you ever engaged?" went on the Imperial catechist: and the incorrigible joker of the Light Dragoons answered quite solemnly: "In some slight actions, Sire, such as the battle of Cross Causeway, and the affair of Moredun Mill". And not until then, on observing the expression of Lord Cathcart's face, did he manage somehow to turn the conversation.

Scott was grieved at *Daisy's* seemingly ungracious change of heart, for it was something new to him. "I have", he had written years before to Miss Seward, "a hereditary attachment to horses—not, I flatter myself, of the common jockey cast, but because I regard them as the kindest and most generous of the subordinate tribes. I hardly even except the dogs: at least they are usually so much better treated that compassion for the steed should be thrown into the scale when we weigh their comparative merits. My wife (a foreigner) never sees horses ill-used without asking what the poor creatures can have done in a state of pre-existence. I would fain hope that they have been carters or hackney-coachmen and are only experiencing a retort of the ill-usage they have formerly inflicted."

*   *   *   *   *

But *Daisy* was right. It was time for the lame Quartermaster, now in middle age, to 'hand over'. The country, at long last, was at peace. As a Poet his reputation was established, and *Waverley* and *Guy Mannering*—though as yet the world knew it not—were signposts on a long road of glorious literary endeavour that was to lead to immortality. There lay before him eleven years of abundance and success; a social radiance to be darkened for the succeeding six by a cloud under whose shadow he was to experience such stress and labour as neither Camp nor Court had ever asked of him. As he quoted bitterly to Lockhart:

While the harness sore galls
And the spurs his side goad,
The high-mettled racer's a hack on the road.

And a hack, in his own estimation only, he was to remain
from that sad day in Castle Street when he greeted Skene,
his faithful confidant and brother Officer, with: "My
friend, give me a shake of your hand—mine is that of a
beggar!", until that sunnier morning in 1831 at Naples,
when, having heard from England that his debts had been
paid in full by his own exertions, he told Sir William Gell
that he was "much relieved"; adding "for I could never
have slept straight in my coffin till I had satisfied every
claim against me".

The Quartermaster of Light Dragoons had 'adjusted'
his last and heaviest account.

But, throughout his life, his cavalry soldiering had been
an inspiration to him as a writer. The rattle of squadrons,
the trumpet-calls, the interaction of sword and bridle
hands, the confidence in danger bred of good-comradeship
and discipline, are all recurring *motifs* in his poems and
novels, the appreciation of which by soldiers gave him
more gratification than all the eulogies in the *Quarterly* or
the *Review*. A military instinct was quintessent in his
psychology. In 1810 his most earnest desire (abandoned in
deference to his wife's alarmed objections) was to "go out
to the Peninsula and take a peep at Lord Wellington and
his merry men"; and he wrote with envy of the luck of his
friend John Miller, K.C., of Lincoln's Inn, who spent the
long vacation of that year with a Highland Regiment

and, with a borrowed musket, fought with them at Busaco.

> O set me on a foreign land
> With my good sword intil my hand,
> And the King's command to fight or die,
> And show me the man that can daunton me!

In the previous year he had read with joy letters from an old brother Officer and still older friend—by then Sir Adam Fergusson and Captain in the 58th Foot (now the 2nd Battalion Northamptonshire Regiment). In one he was told: "I was so fortunate as to get a reading of *The Lady of the Lake* when in the lines of Torres Vedras . . . and my attempts to do justice to the grand opening of the stag-hunt were always followed by bursts of applause—for this canto was the favourite among the rough sons of the fighting Third Division". And in another (communicated second-hand to Scott) Sir Adam related how, when posted with his company on a point of ground exposed to the enemy's artillery, he ordered his men to lie down, and, kneeling himself, read aloud to them the battle in Canto VI; and the listening soldiers only interrupted him by cheers when the shot struck the bank above them. It was not unnatural, then, that Scott should send his first-born son into the Service, from entering which his own lifelong disability had debarred him. But first the lad must do an apprenticeship-in-arms in the same mounted branch of the Auxiliary Forces as his father had. And when, at seventeen, young Walter clanked into the dining-room at Abbotsford in the full panoply of his new Yeomanry uniform, the ex-

Quartermaster kissed him with pride and said: "You are a man. I thought you were my little boy, but I was wrong. It's strange to have a big cavalryman for a son, all of a sudden." His father had seen to it that young Walter— 'Gilnockie' was his nickname in the Abbotsford circle— should be a fine horseman from his earliest years; so that after a creditable career at Sandhurst, he crossed to Ireland to join the 15th (King's) Hussars—Coleridge's old corps—the regiment which he ultimately commanded as Lieutenant-Colonel. Sir Walter Scott the Second died at sea, on his way home on sick-leave from India in 1847.

Scott loved soldiering—its *camaraderie*, its cheeriness, its grumbling, even its rough epithets and engaging profanity in bivouac and billet. In a generation when 'damns' had not yet had their day, when Poets and Prime Ministers, Judges and Commanders-in-Chief interlarded their casual talk with oaths and imprecations, he was remarkable for personal abstention from a habit which with affectionate tolerance he condoned in others. But in an invalid old age, feeble and half dozing in his wheeled-chair while noting up his diary, he would dream himself back on *Brown Adam* with the Light Dragoons again. And it is not impossible that it was a dim vestige of troop-talk during some chilly interlude on parade at Drylaw Mains which lingered in his still humorous memory when, after the tedium of sitting to a sculptor all through an icy January day in 1832, the ex-Quartermaster scribbled faintly in his journal, for all posterity to read, the unusual entry—"*Bloody cold work!*"

WALTER SAVAGE LANDOR

Coronel DE LA INFANTERÍA DEL EJÉRCITO REAL
DE ESPAÑA

EL CORONEL

I

WAR TO THE KNIFE

Con Latín rocín y florín andarás el mundo

ON the evening of the 8th of August 1808 there was a din of conversation in the crowded public rooms of the 'Killigrew Arms', the principal inn of Falmouth. At that time, it is true, in every town of the United Kingdom men were discussing excitedly the news from Spain, but nowhere was the amazing effort of the Spanish people to rid themselves of French domination canvassed with more interest and enthusiasm than in the Cornish port whence for a century and more the famous packets of His Majesty's Post Office had carried mails and passengers to the Spanish Atlantic Ports, the Spanish Main, and Spanish South America.

Three months had passed since the epic events of the *Dos de Mayo* in Madrid had first stirred public feeling throughout Great Britain into sympathy with the heroism of Pedro Velarde and Luis Daoiz, and to execration of Murat's ruthless massacres in the Plaza de Palacio—recorded in all their horror for posterity in the etchings of Goya. And just afterwards had followed the magical 'seven days', during which by what seemed almost supernatural

149

agency the fiery cross of national insurrection had flamed from end to end of the Peninsula—where, even then, the system of internal communications was the worst in Europe. From the Rock of Calpe to the Rio Bidassoa, from Valencia to the marches of Portugal, each district had almost instantaneously produced its Administrative Junta to mobilize every item of its human and material resources against the brutality of the invader. The men and women of Spain, from Grandee to *muletero*, from *duquesa* to dancing-girl, took in a night, as it seemed, their places in the ranks of a simultaneous national resistance. Weapons were scarce, and of money there was even less; but, in a literal sense impossible elsewhere, it was to be *Guerra á Cuchillo*— War to the Knife. In June had begun the incredible defence of Zaragoza by José de Palafox, with a priest and a couple of farm-hands as his chiefs of Staff and a small garrison of townsmen and their womenfolk—including Maria Augustin, *Childe Harold's* 'Maid of Saragossa', who continued to serve the gun still spattered with her lover's blood—against the assaults of Napoleon's hitherto resistless veterans. This was to be no campaign directed by politicians and carried out by professional soldiery, but the first example in modern history of a whole people in arms in defence of its own existence. Carlos IV, the King-abdicant, was a pensioner of the French Government at Compiègne, while his son Ferdinand was confined in Talleyrand's château at Valençay, and the Spanish regular troops had been expatriated to reinforce the French armies in Central Europe. But the very rocks and stones of Spain cried out against the French atrocities, and Murat, beneath whose spurred heel the capital was writhing, took care to keep an escort of his Light Cavalry standing by their horses day and night at the Palacio Real ready for duty with Joseph Buonaparte's travelling carriage.

And now had come news that set Falmouth and all England in a ferment of enthusiasm: Dupont and twenty thousand Frenchmen had surrendered to Castaños and his *guerrilleros* at Baylen in Andalusia; and, what appealed especially to Falmouth ears, the captain of the incoming packet from Gibraltar reported that Sir Hew Dalrymple, the Governor of the Rock, had left to take command against Junot in Portugal; and that off the mouth of the Mondego the packet had passed transports carrying Sir Arthur Wellesley and his little expeditionary force from Ireland to 'an unknown destination'. The air was thick with rumour and speculation. Boney himself was marching south with two hundred thousand men; Sir John Moore and his brigades had been recalled from Sweden and were going out at once; Sir Harry Burrard had been sent for from Calshot Castle, and the quays of the eastern channel ports were heaped high with munitions for the brave Spaniards who, alone among continental peoples, had proved that the French were not invincible. At Westminster, Whigs and Tories were for once at one on the question of practical aid for them. "Hitherto", Mr. Sheridan had declaimed a few nights since in the House of Commons, "Buonaparte has contended with princes without dignity, numbers without ardour, and peoples without patriotism. He has yet to learn what it is to combat a nation with one spirit against him!" And in sonorous antiphon from the Treasury Bench the voice of Canning agreed that "never had so happy an opportunity existed for Britain to strike a bold stroke for the rescue of the world!" Metaphor ran riot in the excited conversation at the Falmouth inn. Was the 'Spanish Ulcer' already developing symptoms that might be fatal to France? Was this cloud in the west on Buonaparte's horizon a warning to him to prepare his chariot? Was the map of Europe, rolled up so ruefully after Austerlitz by the dying Pitt, about to unroll itself? Such were the questions that flew tumultuously from mouth to mouth among the company at the 'Killigrew Arms' as, with an even louder clatter, a chaise and pair galloped up the 'One Street' and stopped at the door. Three travellers, with only hand luggage, it was observed, leapt out and at once were heard in vociferous discussion with the landlord, who, sailing-list in hand, was trying to explain to them that the packet for Corunna had left two hours ago and that a week must pass before the next one sailed. Anger and disappointment rose high in their voices as the three men walked raging into the coffee-room and demanded food and drink; for, it appeared, they had posted day and night from as far east as Brighton to catch the boat for Spain. Two of them, from their accent and the names of O'Hara and Fitzgerald which they inscribed in the inn-book, were clearly Irishmen. The third and most notable of the party, a big powerfully built man in the early thirties whose fine head and features endorsed the authority of his intolerant eye, was an Englishman. And his impetuous signature in the book was that of Walter Savage Landor.

*　　*　　*　　*　　*

Impulse and action were synonymous with Landor. At Brighton a few hours since, he had suddenly determined to sail at once for Spain; and now, impotent, chafing at the delay, a thing abhorrent to his imperious nature, he must kick his heels in Falmouth for a week. Upstairs in his room he sat down to write to Southey, to whom he owed a letter. For during the short Brighton interlude a bulky envelope, which was still unopened, had arrived for him directed in the poet's well-known writing. Southey was an assiduous correspondent, enclosing from time to time his latest MSS. for Landor's criticism and suggestions. And this particular packet happened to contain the first draft of his epic *Kehama* (which was not finished until two years later). There would be time enough now for the recipient to deal with this to Southey's satisfaction and to explain to his closest confidant his latest lightning plan. The two men had been on terms of intimate friendship since first they had met in similar circumstances at Oxford fifteen years before. Landor had come up to Trinity from a private tutor's in Derbyshire after having been removed from Rugby in consequence of an insubordinate altercation with the headmaster on the subjects of bullying and a Latin quantity—with regard to both of which, as it turned out, Landor was in the right. Southey, a year senior, was at Balliol after having been expelled from Westminster for his participation (which took the mild form of an anti-flogging article in the school magazine) in the rebellion against Vincent the great headmaster. Within a year, Landor had been sent down for firing a charge of buck-shot through the window of some High Tory under-graduate, and Southey had left Oxford to join Coleridge and Lovell in their fantastic plan of founding a 'Pantiso-cratic republic' on the banks of the Susquehanna. For, like most young Radicals of their day, the two men had drunk deep draughts of Rousseau and of the heady Jacobin spirit then being distilled in Paris. Both were ardently repub-lican, but with this difference: born with a silver spoon in his mouth, Landor was a pagan and an aristocrat in revolt against monarchy, for which he would substitute a republic on the classic model; he believed with a Roman certitude in aristocratic humanism and legal theory, while Southey's milder bourgeois soul was moved by a Christian com-passion for the sufferings of the poor. His nature was gentler and more malleable than Landor's and reacted more easily to the influence of immediate companions and sur-roundings; so that his republicanism did not long survive his settling down at Keswick to a successful literary career, and was finally drowned in the official butt of sherry that accompanied his appointment to the Laureateship.

But the two men cherished a lifelong devotion to each other, though Landor remained a patrician democrat to the end—in Carlyle's phrase "an unsubduable Roman, whose words sound like the ring of legionaries' swords on the helmets of barbarians". Since 1798, when he had pub-

lished *Gebir*, his long Miltonic poem—a brave foreshadow-
ing of the Landor to come—he had written nothing, but
had been wandering to and fro between Bath and Wells,
Bristol and Warwick, Paris and London, possessed by a
demon of unrest and unproductiveness. In Paris six years
ago he had met the First Consul—"an ungenerous, un-
gentlemanly, unmanly Corsican"—who had aroused at
once his instinctive misgiving and dislike. Since then had
come the Empire, and the shadow of Napoleon began to
stretch across the Channel. A creature of the glorious
Revolution, a potential harbinger of the revival of Roman
republicanism, Buonaparte had proved himself to be a
traitor, and the triple consulate a foul conspiracy against
Liberty. The Tribune had become a tyrant, acclaimed by
the very people whose ideals he had subverted; the Peace
of Tilsit had confirmed the menace of the 18th Brumaire.
Buonaparte had crushed the Germans, made satellites of
the Russians, and was now scheming to subjugate Spain
and Portugal. The French had betrayed the cause of Freedom and were closing the avenues to universal redemption
which they had opened in 1793. Here was a nation which,
though it had initiated the greatest progressive political
movement in modern history, yet was capable in the course
of a few years of becoming the bully of Europe at the
behest of an overrated adventurer, a pervert from the
principles of 'the Rights of Man' who did not hesitate to
drench a continent in blood to achieve his reactionary
objects.

And now the Spanish people were standing up to the

bully, like the small boys whom Landor had championed in the past at Rugby. Moreover, Landor was above all an Englishman, and was moved to his depths by the French threat to England. For once he was in accord with the mass feeling of his countrymen and even with the fighting fervour of the aristocratic military caste whom he detested. On his leaving Oxford his godfather General Powell—a veteran of the American War and an ex-governor of Gibraltar—had offered to obtain him a Cornetcy if he would suppress his republican views; and Landor had indignantly refused. He was a republican in times when the avowal of such a creed implied a definite moral cast and involved social ostracism. So detested had he made himself by the expression of his opinions in his native town of Warwick, that when his brother (who was courting the Colonel's daughter) had tried to arrange for his being given a commission in the County Militia, the Second-in-Command had openly declared in mess: "If young Walter Landor gets a commission in this regiment, I shall resign my own!"—a sentiment most cordially endorsed by his brother Officers. But if he would not seek a commission in the monarchist army of his own country, Landor determined to prove his detestation of the French by fighting with the Spaniards. He had ample means: he was his own master. He would offer his sword and his money to the people of Spain. At Brighton he had heard that a Falmouth packet was sailing for Corunna on August the 8th, and with his two recruits he had posted the whole width of the south coast only to miss it by two hours. No matter. Here was such stuff for a letter to Southey as he had never yet written. He pictured the poet acclaiming his passionate action to the Keswick circle, while shaking a mistrustful head over the headlong Landorian method of achieving it. "Nothing that I do," he wrote, "will create much surprise in those who know my character. I am going to Spain. In three days I shall have sailed!" (A sanguine anticipation of the scheduled time!) "At Brighton one evening I preached a crusade to two auditors. Inclination was not wanting, and in a few minutes everything was fixed. I am now about to express a wish at which your gentler and more benevolent soul will shudder. May every Frenchman out of France perish! May the Spaniards not spare one! No calamities can chain them down from their cursed monkey-tricks; no generosity can bring back to their remembrance that a little while since they mimicked, till they really thought themselves, free men. Detestable race, profaners of re-publicanism! Since the earth will not open to swallow them all up, may even kings partake of the glory of their utter extermination! I am learning night and day the Spanish language. I ought not to give my opinion of it at present, but I confess it appears to me such as I should have expected to hear spoken by a Roman slave sulky from the bastinado! I hope to join the Spanish Army immedi-ately on my landing, and I wish only to fight as a private soldier. There is nothing in this unless it could be known what I have left for it, and, having left, have lost!"

The letter dispatched, with others to his lawyers and his bankers, Landor spent the remainder of the seven days in annotating Southey's embryonic epic, in wrestling with his Spanish grammar, in supplementing his inadequate outfit from the shops in the port, and in taking long furious walks —southward to Constantine and Helford, or north to Redruth and Truro—sometimes accompanied by the two Irishmen, but more often alone; for they found the time pass more pleasantly in the taprooms of the quayside taverns or in dalliance with the local fair than in company with this "deep-mouthed Bœotian Savage" with his unceasing fulminations against Kings and Consuls and his impetuous energy which walked them off their legs.

But at last came the day of sailing, and the three of them with their scanty gear were bundled into a dinghy to be rowed out with the mail-bags to the packet lying ready for sea off Trefusis Point. And soon the anchor was short up, the sails began to swell on the swaying masts, and land and shipping to glide by on either side of the slow-moving hull. The Spanish adventure had begun.

II

AT THE AYUNTAMIENTO

Guerra, caza y amores,
Por un placer mil dolores

A BRISK north-easter sang in the halyards as it hustled the
packet through the white tide-rip of the Carrick Roads
until St. Mawes and St. Anthony's faded behind her into
the summer haze. On she ran before the friendly breeze,
past the dreaded Manacles and Helford estuary until the
measureless waste of the Atlantic glimmered and glinted
ahead. Landor and the two Irishmen stood near the helms-
man and watched the skipper, Captain Atkins, and his
bo'sun superintending the clearing of the little guns and
the due ordering of the stands of muskets, cutlasses, and
boarding-pikes. The Corunna packet was a 200-ton brig
like most of her sisters; (a few were square-topsailed cutters
or brigantines, and two of the West India and Brazil boats
were full-rigged). She carried a crew of twenty-five, with
an armament of some small six-pounders, and, as stern-
chaser, a long nine-pounder carronade of the special Post-
Office pattern. For all down the long sea-chord of the
Biscay arc from Finistère in Brittany to Finisterra in north-
western Spain the French privateers were a menace to

British shipping, the Falmouth packets being their favourite quarry. The packet-skippers had orders never to fight if it could be avoided, and their fast handy vessels could usually show a clean pair of heels to any Frenchman. But the skippers of the Cherbourg *chasse-marée* and the big Breton luggers out of Brest and Quimper vied with those of the Girondais letters-of-marque and the armed Basque whalers from St. Jean de Luz in trying for a Falmouth prize. And all of these were just then burning to avenge the disgrace of the previous winter, when Captain Bill Rogers of the West India packet *Windsor Castle* (with a crew of twenty-eight), having failed to outsail the *Jeanne Richard* of Cherbourg (with a crew of ninety-two), had greeted the French boarding-party with his nine-pounder crammed to the muzzle with grape and musket-balls, and had followed up the convulsion by leaping with his men over the enemy's bulwarks. With naked fist and cutlass the Englishmen had driven the crew below and battened them down, so that the *Windsor Castle* brought her prize in triumph to Bridgetown in the Barbadoes, having lost but three men killed to the enemy's twenty-one.

To Landor, however, the seas seemed clear enough both of Frenchmen and foul weather, until on the second night the fickle wind veered round and rose to gale force from the opposite quarter. The Irishmen took to their berths and lay groaning in the thunderous darkness, though next day there was a dead calm, and the ship, with sagging sails, rolled idly in the trough of the seas. Landor raged up and down the heaving deck, his passionate energy inflamed by this inaction forced on him by the elements. He grumbled unceasingly about the weather and the ship, which, in truth, was leaky and disgracefully ill-found. The tea was bad, the water worse; there were no lemons, and what fruit there was was rotten. Captain Atkins was irritable and apprehensive of attack, and on the fourth evening, sure enough, they sighted a larger vessel which was undoubtedly a French privateer. But Fate relented, for a slant of rising wind and the gathering darkness enabled the packet to draw off unmolested. But the alternate storm and calm continued and, after making her landfall off Cape Ortegal, for forty-eight hours the little ship was the sport of the big Atlantic rollers within a couple of miles of the jagged coastline of Galicia, before, on the eighth day out from home, battered and with damaged rigging she managed somehow to crawl into Corunna Harbour.

No time was to be lost. Landor and his two companions, the first volunteers from Great Britain for the Spanish National Army, scrambled impatiently up the landing-steps without more than the briefest adieux to Captain Atkins—to whom, however, Landor some three months later sent the present of a compass as a memento of "the pleasant and instructive hours spent in his company on the voyage". (The Captain was to lose his life during the ensuing spring, when his packet was on dispatch service under Lord Gambier, who was then blockading the French fleet in Aix Roads.)

But the faces which the three adventurers saw around them on the *embarcadero* were scarcely expressive of Sunny

Spain. Here were no gay *caballeros* and vivacious *señoritas*, but men and women wearing an air of resolution, grim as the rugged background of their Galician hills, that seemed to testify to their implacable purpose.

Charles Stuart, a rising young diplomatist, had been sent out to Corunna some weeks previously by the Foreign Office to ascertain the practicable requirements of the Juntas; and with him was Charles Richard Vaughan of the same Service, who had been a fellow of All Souls and a junior to Landor at Rugby. By dint of such Spanish as Landor had been able to acquire from grammar and dictionary the trio found their way at last to the English envoy's lodgings; only to be met by Vaughan, who with many apologies told them that Stuart had left a few hours before on a secret mission, and that he himself was starting immediately for Laregovia. Having with some difficulty procured rooms for himself and the Irishmen, Landor proceeded forthwith to write in the vilest schoolboy Spanish to the Governor, Don Alfonso Alvedo, offering their services and on his own behalf the sum of ten thousand reals to pay the expenses of as many men, "though a thousand in number", as might be ready to march at once with them to join the Spanish forces in north-eastern Galicia. He also enclosed a draft for a further ten thousand reals for relief work at Venturada, a town recently burnt by the French.

On receipt of the letter Alvedo sent for Landor, and with his warmest thanks informed him that it and the money had at once been forwarded to the Superior Council of Castile; that he accepted most gratefully Landor's offer to march the volunteers, and with the local Junta would make all necessary preparations without delay. A few days later Stuart returned to Corunna, and it was arranged that at the next meeting of the Junta he should introduce Landor and officially approve his offer on behalf of the British Government. Meanwhile the three volunteers from England became the darlings of the local notables, who, led by a certain Don Benito de Novoa, did their utmost to express their appreciation in practical form.

But Landor's fiery impatience chafed at this procrastination of his plans against the 'profaners of republicanism'; and he busied himself mustering and fitting out his motley volunteers and planning his route of march with Stuart; though Don Alfonso, and Count Gimondi, president of the local Junta, kept open house for him, and the venerable Bishop of Orense waited on him in stately recognition of his munificence to Venturada. Presently, too, he received from the Superior Council a communication in ornate Castilian, in which the Doyen, Señor Arias Mon, after many ceremonious compliments, informed him that his offer to equip and march a draft for the forces in the field had been duly received through Don Alfonso and was most gratefully accepted; and that Don Pedro Cevallos, the Minister for Foreign Affairs and War, begged the writer to express to the Señor Landor the high sense entertained by the Council of his generosity, valour, and enthusiasm.

So that all was now ready for the draft to march, and nothing remained but the final formalities with the Junta. Accordingly, on his last evening in Corunna, Landor was ushered by Stuart into the *Ayuntamiento* (Town Hall) where this democratic committee of public safety—composed of grandees and farmers, stevedores and ships' captains, and even bull-fighters—was then in session with Count Gimondi in the chair. And the Envoy—in French, for his Spanish was independable—introduced his countryman, expatiated on his contribution of funds and personal service, and on behalf of His Britannic Majesty's Government warmly endorsed these disinterested offerings to the Spanish cause. Stuart spoke at length, and as he boomed on and on Landor sat restless for the road, and after the first few minutes hardly troubling to listen to this prosy reiteration to Cervantes' countrymen of his own Quixotic qualities.

And then, in an instant, occurred a misunderstanding so puerile as scarcely to be credible, an imbroglio of quite amazing irrationality, which could never have arisen except in connection with a man of Landor's violent and unreasoning impetuosity. Having concluded his eulogy of Landor before the bored subject of it had appreciated the fact, Stuart incautiously took the occasion to deal with another matter—quite alien to Landor and his offer, and relative to a Spanish official who had recently arrived in Corunna on his way to Monte Video, and who, on information now proved to be false, had been arrested by the Junta as a traitor in the pay of France. In his official capacity the English Envoy had, for some reason, become involved in this proceeding, and with Don Benito de Novoa had established the *bona fides* of the suspect. He now appealed to Novoa to corroborate his statement that the unfortunate prisoner was innocent and owed his position merely to his imprudent behaviour since arrival in the port; and that, so far from being glutted with French gold, the man, in fact, had no money at all. *"Il est fou,"* explained Stuart finally, with contemptuous commiseration, *"il n'a pas d'argent."*

For ten minutes Landor had not been listening: this last emphatic sentence alone recaptured his attention.

He sprang to his feet at once. *He* was mad, was he? A mercenary impostor! This then was the sneering peroration of a speech whose beginning had bored him with its long-drawn but now quite obviously sarcastic commendation!

It was the old story! Knowing his republican opinions, this minion of a monarchical government—acting, doubtless, on instructions—had fooled him to the top of his bent and now had thrown off the mask and was trying to disparage his action to the Junta and to vilify him as a crazy and impecunious adventurer. His face contorted with rage, his huge frame shaking with passionate resentment, Landor thundered in fiery French to the astonished Junta. He called High Heaven to witness that he "could yearly and with no inconvenience save sufficient for the accomplishment of every offer he had made, and that he could not apply it with more lasting joy to any other purpose than the advancement of the cause of the Spanish people against tyranny! A letter of the Superior Council was in his pocket, and his intention remained unaltered to reach Blake's camp and to conduct to headquarters the men entrusted to his care in time for the expected battle!" A syllable or two would have sufficed to correct his misapprehension; but not a word of explanation did he demand from the astonished Stuart. Without so much as a glance in his direction Landor stalked from the council-chamber leaving the Junta breathless and dumbfounded.

* * * * *

Crabbe Robinson has recorded the opinion of an Italian guest of Landor's at the Villa Gherardesca at Fiesole: "All Englishmen are mad; but this one——!"

There were two parts to the man's anomalous nature. That nearest the surface, and therefore more easily apparent and remembered, is represented in this amazing incident. It falls into line with the shot-gun episode at Oxford, the law-suits with his neighbours and his tenantry, the thrashing of his solicitor, the challenge to the diplomat at Leghorn for daring to whistle in the street as Mrs. Landor passed, the setting sail for France—alone in an open oyster-boat—after a quarrel with her, the throwing out of the window of his cook in Florence, and the levelling of his mansion at Llanthony to the ground. The other part expressed itself in his love of flowers, his tenderness with children, his devotion to his dog. Leigh Hunt, who had experience of both aspects of his character, compared him to "a stormy mountain pine that should produce lilies".

III

LEON AND THE ASTURIAS

Quien va á la guerra las Nagas aguarda

THE draft paraded at dawn. Landor, still burning at Stuart's imagined insult, stuck to his word given in August to Southey and marched as a private soldier in the ranks, though actually the commander. During the past few weeks he had worked in the preparations with all the iron devotion of which he was capable, arranging the forward rationing and billets, and supervising the distribution of the heterogeneous armoury that had been collected at Corunna—muskets, a blunderbuss or two, and an assortment of antiquated swords and pistols. There was no question of uniforms: fortunately the Gallegan peasant is inured to hardship; his *manta* of blanketing serves him for a cloak or bedding, and his *alpargatas* are the best kind of marching boots for him. O'Hara and Fitzgerald were of the company; but from this point onward their names disappear from any record. They were of that vast multitude of the 'walking gentlemen' of history who emerge into the limelight and cross the stage for a brief moment during the drama of some great man's life, and then, their usefulness exhausted, are seen no more.

The first objective of the march was Lugo, an old walled town on the main road that leads south-eastward to Madrid. Here they were billeted at a *posada* just outside the walls, and waited some days for the arrival of other drafts. Stuart was to have rejoined Landor here, but, as he afterwards explained, was detained in Corunna. Had he appeared, the whole misunderstanding might have been righted. As it was, Landor was convinced that Stuart dared not face him.

But the place appealed to Landor; for he knew it to have been the Roman *Lucus Augusti*, the capital of Lusitania, the last province of Roman Spain to be settled and latinized and to be administered as military territory direct from Rome. Here, too, he met Broderick, an English staff-officer on special service who had been asked by Stuart to look out for him, and whose opinion of Blake, the British Commander of the Galician army, occasioned him grave misgivings. During the stay at Lugo the draft, headed by Landor, helped to extinguish a serious fire that broke out in the neighbourhood of a supply dump of provisions collected from the country round to save them from the looting of the French cavalry. The men brought sacks of earth and buckets of water from the Minho, here as wide as a lake, and managed to save the food; and Landor received the official thanks of the local authorities.

Then on they marched, through Basside and Nocera and lovely Castel de Los Moros with its park-like meadows, to Villafranca in Leon; and from here Landor sent a letter to Vaughan, whom Broderick had reported then to be in

Madrid, giving him an account of the Stuart episode. "Forbearance I have shown," he wrote, "and even this letter will controvert the charge of imbecility as surely as the same charge would be proved by whatever is intemperate and coarse. The 10,000 reals (why am I forced to mention them?) which I paid into the hands of the government at Corunna and a daily allowance of full pay to every soldier I am leading to the armies, together with some occasional gratuities to keep up their spirits on the march, are presumptive proof that the calculations of Mr. Stuart are groundless, frivolous, and false!" And not content with trying to vindicate himself to his old schoolfellow, he wrote a wildly intemperate note to Stuart himself, copies of which, without waiting for a reply from his supposed traducer, he sent to friends in Corunna with directions to have them printed in Spanish and English for public circulation.

On through Leon trekked the Landorian legion, now swollen with drafts which had come in at every halting-place, over the southern spurs of the Cantabrian chain to Aguilar in the Asturias; and here Landor handed over his men, who were at once absorbed into a division of Blake's army.

But at last he was under fire, though only in outpost affairs and brushes with enemy patrols. For the General, distrustful of his raw levies and sick at heart at the losing fight before him, refused to commit himself to any offensive measures. And the situation was indeed disheartening for all who were pledged to the Spanish cause. Roliça and

Vimiero had been won by Wellesley, but the armistice signed with Kellermann by the trio of British commanders in an interval during their bickerings over seniority had developed into the Convention of Cintra, under which the French were permitted to evacuate Portugal and to be shipped back to France at the expense of His Majesty's Government, while they were left a free hand in Spain. As a result, the flood of the *Grande Armée* was sweeping King Joseph back again to Madrid; and Sir John Moore in Leon with the British Expeditionary Force from Portugal was in danger of being cut off. It was now October and the autumn rains were threatening; the Spanish fought sullenly at Reynosa for the control of the Asturian pass; and in the retirement on the northern ports Landor found himself at Bilbao, "serving three launches with muskets and powder, after carrying a child three miles that was too heavy for its exhausted mother". Moreover, the Gallegos and Asturians were losing heart, and every nightfall saw hundreds skulking back to save their homes. Charles Stuart, now acting Envoy in Madrid, was sending frantic messages to Moore to come and defend the capital; and, harassed as he was, yet found time to write at length to Landor and to Vaughan the fullest explanations of the Corunna episode.

The position in the Asturias seemed definitely hopeless; and Landor, despairing of further help for Spain from England and regarding his own efforts as wasted by Blake's lack of the offensive spirit and by the treachery at Cintra, determined to return. He would devote his pen, his influence, his money to agitating for a denouncement of

the Convention. A convenient fishing-boat took him back
to Corunna from Bilbao, along a panorama of the grey
Asturian mountains already snow-capped and seeming to
hang between sea and sky, and beneath them the Cantabrian coast, vine-clad to the sea, with white villages dotted
among the foot-hills like fruit upon a wall, and with a
frieze of chestnut woods above them, topped by a parapet
of pines.

And, as though fickle Fortune wished to compensate him
in October for her scurvy trick in August, a Falmouth
packet homeward bound was waiting in the harbour.

When he watched *La Tierra de la Maria Santissima* re-
ceding gradually astern his memories of its *guerilleros*, its
grave and kindly noblemen and peasants, its varied scenery
—sunlit and fertile or arid and austere—would seem to
have graven themselves indelibly on Landor's mind. For in
Count Julian, the Spanish tragedy which he began to write
within a year or so, his march-route is perpetuated . . .

> If strength be wanted for security,
> Mountains the guard forbidding all approach
> With iron-pointed and uplifted gales,
> Thou wilt be welcome too in Aguilar,
> Impenetrable, marble-turreted,
> Surveying from aloft the limpid ford,
> The massive farm, the sylvan avenue;
> Whose hospitality I proved myself,
> A willing leader in no impious cause
> When fame and Freedom urged me; or mayst dwell
> In Reynosa's dry and thriftless dale
> Unharvested beneath October moons,
> Among those frank and cordial villagers.

IV

EL CORONEL

El mas letrado no es el mas sabio

AT home again in England Landor found that the country
was ringing with a popular outcry against the Cintra Convention. The signatory Generals must be tried by court-
martial! Somebody must be shot—or hung and drawn and
quartered! There was no need of his leonine roar to supple-
ment the invective of Canning and the fulminations of
Cobbett, the reprobation even of the gentle Wordsworth
and the now mellowing Southey. And so, physically
fatigued and mentally dejected, yet in a curious mood of
tired tranquillity, he would seem to have decided that
there was nothing left for him during the gradually
darkening days of early winter but to content himself
with writing copiously to Southey in the intervals of opening his accumulated letters. And some of these, though
then he seems to have taken but small account of them,
are not without interest now—especially those which bore
the Spanish postmark.

There was one, for instance, from Vaughan in which the
future ambassador to Washington enclosed another written
to him by Stuart and dated "Madrid: The 18th October",

from which the following is an extract: "Don Benito de Novoa will certify that Mr. Landor must have misunderstood me, and that the language he alludes to could not have been directed against him. On the contrary, I cited Mr. Landor's handsome offer as a proof of the goodwill and enthusiasm which animates Englishmen; and knowing from you the talents, fortune, and character of that gentleman, I should have been mad or a fool had I been base enough to depreciate his exertions in so good a cause, who have myself descended from my own rank in the Service to engage heartily in favour of Spanish liberty on Spanish ground. You were the bearer of a message to Mr. Landor expressing our regret for our departure at the moment of his arrival in Corunna; and afterwards the same circumstance in Lugo would not permit me to show him the civilities I desired. I would willingly have furnished him with such recommendations to the Army as I could give him; and I actually requested General Broderick when he passed through Lugo to forward his efforts in the cause of Spain by every facility which his situation at headquarters could command."

And there was one from the Envoy himself dated "Aranjuez: the 14th of November", in answer to Landor's note from Lugo in September: "I learn with much regret that I have had the misfortune unintentionally to offend you at Corunna, and I hasten to clear up a mistake which appears to have given rise to sentiments in your mind very different from those I have always entertained respecting yourself since I witnessed your conduct in this country.

I can assure you that I do not recollect the conversation you state to have passed between myself and Don Benito de Novoa the evening I saw you in the Junta; and I solemnly declare upon my honour that if such expressions fell from my lips they neither applied to you nor to any friend of yours. I could not oppose or calumniate an undertaking which every motive of interest and zeal called on me to support: nor is it compatible with my character to hold language to the personal prejudice of any Englishman, knowing it to be false. I could not be ignorant of your talents, which are manifested in writings well received by the world and were evident from your conversation: our mutual friend Mr. Vaughan bore testimony to your fortune and rank in life; and your character was fully proved by your exertions in favour of Spain. I was myself embarked in the same cause, and having been commissioned by Government to ascertain the wants of the Spaniards and to transmit them particulars of every description until an Envoy should be appointed, is it likely that I should counteract the zeal of others labouring to the same purpose? Though I never made a merit of language in your favour at the time, I feel now compelled to tell you that I have repeatedly desired the Junta of Corunna to hold up your conduct as an example to other individuals equally well disposed. The distance of Galicia will not allow me to send you the assurance of Don Benito de Novoa that such is the case; but I transmit the copy of a letter from the President of that Junta who was present on the day that you allude to, which (notwithstanding his mistakes) will prove the truth of my assertions. I have also written to Vaughan at Laregovia, who I doubt not will do the same. If however their letters are not sufficient to show that I am incapable of animosity to a person engaged in such a cause, I presume you will be convinced by the enclosed answer from the Minister of Foreign Affairs to a note I transmitted to the Central Junta detailing the service you have rendered to Spain. Honorary rank in their army can be no object to one in your situation; and though it is the only mode of distinction hitherto conferred on any Englishman by the central government, I should have declined their offer had not the consideration that you may like a character giving you a right to repair to the headquarters of their armies when you please induced me rather to wait for your determination. When Mr. Vaughan returns to Madrid on his way home I shall request him to deliver to you the original letters which I have passed on the subject, and if they are satisfactory, I hope I may look forward to shake hands with you as a well-wisher of that country wherever we meet."

Such was the characteristically long-winded self-defence of the good-hearted and much harassed Envoy, written with care and feeling at a time when his official position was one of the gravest anxiety, with Napoleon at the very gate of Madrid. Landor, with curt ill-grace, accepted the proffered olive-branch; and he wrote to Southey later: "Mr. Stuart has declared that he never could apply those expressions to me that I resented, and offers peace. I always accept this offer." With him the incident had dwindled into triviality. It was only a parenthesis in the troublous tale of his life and he showed no sense at all of the insane injustice of his own conduct to Stuart.

The enclosure from Cevallos, the Spanish Foreign Minister, intimated that it was proposed to confer the rank of Colonel in the Spanish Army upon the Señor Landor as an official token of the gratitude to him of the Spanish Government and people for his services. And in the following month the commission actually arrived, together with a letter couched in terms of the warmest appreciation and a special copy of the *Gaceta de Madrid* containing the notification, "Coronel de la Infantería del Ejército Real de España". Thus within five months did Landor leap from the rank of private to that of Colonel: and a Colonel he remained for the next six years, until King Ferdinand on his triumphant return to Madrid in 1814 abrogated the liberal Constitution of 1812, dissolved the Cortes, and reverted to absolutism. And then it was that Landor returned the commission and the letters to Don Pedro with a fiery note saying that while he had been willing to aid a people in the assertion of its liberties against "the antagonist of Europe" he would have nothing to do with "a perjured and traitorous king"!

(In 1815, so Howitt relates, when Landor happened to be in Tours, he saw a dusty travelling-chaise drive into the town, with a single servant in the rumble and containing a pale fat little man in a shabby overcoat. Hating and despising as he did "the antagonist of Europe", Landor made his way alongside the vehicle and spoke quietly through the window. "You are not safe here," he whispered; "I see through your disguise—and others may!" "Monsieur," replied a tired voice from within, "you are, I perceive, an Englishman. My secret is in good keeping." And, touching an incongruously civilian hat, the lonely traveller drove on, taking the road that ran southward to Rochefort—and the *Bellerophon*.)

Charles Stuart died in 1845, a Peer and a Privy Councillor, after having been Ambassador in Paris and St. Petersburg.

Landor never returned to Spain, though the abiding influence of his Spanish adventure is evident in his writings. For he wrote a volume of comment and advice on Juntas; in 1812 appeared his drama of *Count Julian*, with a Spanish setting and many passages descriptive of places he knew in Galicia and the Asturias; and his *Conversation* between Lacy and Cura Merino deals with King Ferdinand's subversion of the liberal Constitution of Cadiz. But Italy was to be the land of his adoption, and it was there that in later middle-age this 'untamable and Olympian schoolboy', though essentially a Poet, was at last to settle down in his fiftieth year to the production of prose masterpieces, serene and splendid in the stark clarity of their style, which have secured his immortality.

> The gods approve
> The depth, and not the tumult, of the soul.

It was as though Providence, conscious that the development of Landor's genius had been hindered too long by a restless impulse for physical action, had decreed a prolongation of its productive maturity beyond the allotted span. For his literary power continued unabated until the end came in his ninetieth year, not very long after he had penned his own transcendent epitaph:

> I strove with none, for none was worth my strife;
> Nature I loved, and next to Nature, Art;
> I warmed both hands before the fire of Life;
> It sinks, and I am ready to depart.

GEORGE GORDON BYRON
SIXTH BARON BYRON

Brigade-Commander (Archistrategos)
GREEK ARMY OF INDEPENDENCE, 1824

That the thanks of the Committee be communicated to
Lord Byron for his generous offer in service of the Greeks, and
that he be requested to favour us with any suggestions or communications likely to advance the cause.

RESOLUTION OF THE GREEK COMMITTEE IN LONDON

April 26, 1823

The sword, the banner, and the field,
    Glory and Greece around me see!
The Spartan, borne upon his shield
    Was not more free.

Awake! (not Greece—she is awake!)
    Awake my spirit! Think through whom
Thy life-blood tracks its parent lake
    And then strike home!

THE ARCHISTRATEGOS

I

THE CORSAIR OF THE *HERCULES*

The Banner'd pomp of War, the glittering files,
O'er whose gay trappings stern Bellona smiles;
The brazen trump, the spirit-stirring drum
That bid the foe defiance ere they come . . .

AT Argostoli, the chief town of the Ionian island of
Cephalonia, the Officers' Mess of H.M. 8th Foot—now
the King's (Liverpool) Regiment—was gay with lights and
agog with a rare expectancy. From Colonel Duffie, the
C.O., down to the latest-joined Subaltern all the Officers
were in a ferment of expectancy. For this was to be no
ordinary guest-night, with some outlying Resident or Collector as visitor, or some Cephalonian bigwig oppressively
polite in a Graeco-Italian patois which few of his hosts
could understand. The guest of honour this evening was
to be no less a celebrity than the famous—some would
have it infamous—Lord Byron, the poet and profligate,
the voluptuary of Venice, the philanderer turned filibuster,
who, having broken his seven years' exile on the Continent,
was now *en route* to join the Greek insurgents, and whose
corsair-craft, the *Hercules* (a disappointingly bluff-bowed
and prosaic English collier brig), had cast anchor in the
port two days before. In 1823, incredible as it may seem

181

to modern ears, poets could make money and poems prove
to be best-sellers: and with the rest of an earnestly intelligent public most of the Officers of the 8th had read *Childe
Harold*, *The Giaour*, and the earlier cantos of *Don Juan*, and
identified their guest romantically in terms of all three of
his heroes. And here was the notorious genius in person,
coming to dine with them on his way to help overthrow
Turkish despotism in those classic lands whose outline
showed, pencilled clearly every day on their local horizon,
and whose enslaved inhabitants already were hailing him
as a Liberator. A thrilling interlude indeed to break the
normal *ennui* of garrison life at Argostoli! For in spite of
the perfect climate and fine scenery, soldiering in the then
British Protectorate of the Ionian Islands was at best a
boring business. At Argostoli, it is true, there were the
regular calls of sailing-packets, chance visits of British
ships, and an occasional festive welcome to the Fleet from
Malta. But the rest was dull routine; a round of guards
and parades mitigated by excursions to the adjacent islands
of Ithaca and Zante, a dance or two given by the Cephalonian aristocracy (whose girls were pretty but apt to run
to fat), some fishing from feluccas, some sailing-matches
in the long eight miles of the bay, and, with any luck, a
few days' leave for wildfowl-shooting on the mainland—
though, since the Morean rising of 1821, this had become
increasingly hard to obtain owing to the strictness with
which 'King Tom' (for so Sir Thomas Maitland, the
eccentric and autocratic High Commissioner at Corfu, was
universally known) chose to interpret his instructions to

avoid the slightest risk of compromising British neutrality in the struggle between the Greeks and their Turkish masters.

And now, just as the mess-bugle blew, a boat was seen approaching from the *Hercules*, which was moored opposite the lazaretto further down the bay. At once Colonel Duffie, with Colonel Charles Napier, the Resident, and Captain Pitt-Kennedy, the Resident's Secretary, hurried towards the verandah on the bastion to welcome the distinguished guests—for the invitation had included Lord Byron's suite—while the Officers ranged themselves behind in an expectant group. First up the landing-steps came young Hamilton Browne, whom they knew as a protégé of Napier's, recently dismissed from the Ionian Service for his Philhellene proclivities and now Lord Byron's Intelligence Officer: then strode in a towzled giant, Trelawny, with fiercely suspicious eyes and clothes that suggested the deserter from the Royal Navy with a dash of the mountain brigand, a younger version of Millais' portrait of him in *The North-West Passage*. Behind him sidled in a young Italian, small and neatly dressed, with an apprehensive and diffident expression on his effeminate face—Dr. Francesco Bruno, his Lordship's personal physician, without whom he went nowhere. He was followed by a handsome blond-haired young Officer in some sort of uniform, his face white with traces of anxiety (or was it *mal de mer*?) and exhibiting an expression of ineffective conscientiousness with a sort of nebulous charm—this must be Count Pietro Gamba, brother of the Guiccioli and his Lordship's Staff-Officer. And at last the author-hero of *Don Juan* made his entrance; a slightly disappointing *Lara*, with an irresolute and self-conscious smile:

> . . . who not yet was past his manhood's prime
> Though sear'd by toil and something touch'd by Time.

Fair-complexioned and very thin, he had unruly dark-brown hair, a little oily and quite grey at the temples, delicate hands, and small feet of which the deformity was singularly unnoticeable. The head was fine, and the face broad and open, tapering to a firm oval chin; the nose largish and well shaped, with a mobile mouth below a short and sensitive upper lip. Under a loose and romantic boat-cloak he wore ill-cut nankeen overalls, a wide collar with a flowing tie, and a dark-green cavalry jacket, frogged and braided. A tall Italian with earrings and black whiskers followed him as closely as a devoted dog, but remained during dinner outside on the verandah, with one eye on the riding-light of the *Hercules* and the other watchful for his *Lordo Inglese* within: this was clearly Tita Falciere, his Lordship's faithful Venetian gondolier. (In after years, Tita was to become the equally devoted servant of Benjamin Disraeli at Hughenden, where he married Mrs. Disraeli's maid, and eventually became, on the Prime Minister's nomination, a messenger at the India Office.)

Napier greeted Byron warmly and introduced him to Colonel Duffie, who presented his Officers. At table the Poet was placed between the Colonel and the Resident, and his diffident smile and defensive reticence vanished before the sympathetic and spontaneous cordiality of his reception. He was there that evening merely for reasons of policy pressed on him by Napier and Hamilton Browne: for he had sore recollections of the superciliousness of the Officers he had met at Malta on his visit to that island with Hobhouse during his first Mediterranean voyage fourteen years before. His self-consciousness prompted him to imagine that soldiers, as men of action, despised him as a flabby philanderer who happened to have a knack of versifying, and his sensitiveness shrank, in view of all that had since happened, from what he anticipated would be an intensified repetition. From the lampoons and diatribes in the Press and the attitude of the crowds at Dover when he left England, he took it for granted that the tenor of his writings and the scandal of his private affairs—of which he never tired of boasting—had incurred the odium and aversion of all his countrymen, which he affected to despise; and for years his morbid egotism had nurtured within him a kind of persecution-mania which fed his lowering melancholy and lent pungency to the sneers and sarcasms that punctuated his letters. But the Officers of the 8th seemed actually glad and interested to meet him, and his suspicious sulkiness was disarmed by their attentive affability and cheerful talk. He reciprocated, almost volubly; throwing aside his rôle of "the man of mystery and loneliness", and—to Dr. Bruno's stupefaction —even his dyspepsia; for he ate and drank heartily, and even laughed. (Apart from its rarity, Byron's laugh was memorable; "of all his peculiarities", so Hobhouse records, "his laugh is that of which I have the most distinct recollection".) Then came the port: and after the loyal toasts the Colonel proposed that of his health, which the Officers drank standing. As he rose to his feet to reply, fumbling with the scented handkerchief between his fingers, he looked down with emotion at the long perspective of the mess-table between its two fences of scarlet uniforms, its white napery glowing in the soft candlelight with a sheen of glass and silver. Such unexpected *camaraderie* and kindness was unnerving, almost to tears. But he recovered himself in the impulsive presentation of a pose, more genial than his wont but still as mysteriously intriguing. Theatrical even when feeling genuine emotion, he could not resist self-dramatization before so favourable an audience. At Harrow they had ridiculed his traces of a Scots accent, a vestige of his Aberdonian childhood. He would reverse that situation now to these grown-up schoolboys, by the assumption of a superior and world-weary exoticism which should epitomize *Don Juan's* romantic Odyssey and *Childe Harold's* rakish pilgrimage, with all their implications. In an alien staccato which would have done credit to Bruno or Gamba he "begged to thank the Officers sincerely"; stressing the pleasure he felt that evening at finding himself once more in the company of his compatriots, but tendering his regret that he "could not adequately express his sense of obligation since he had been so long in the practice of speaking a foreign language that he was unable easily to convey his sentiments in English".

In his chair once more he whispered to the Colonel,

"Was it a success? Did I say what was required?" Duffie's reply is not on record; but he must have sensed his Officers' politely dissembled deprecation of such obvious attitudinizing. That it didn't 'go down' was quite imperceptible to Byron, whose sensations were wholly those of gratitude and pleasure. Meanwhile, he discussed with the Colonel plans for an immediate trip to Ithaca, and asked about Captain Knox the Resident at Valpy and Mr. Moore the Collector; laughed at stories told by Napier and other Officers about Lieutenant-General 'King Tom', his easy hand and prowess with the port-decanter and his iron hand with recalcitrant Greek skippers at Corfu; and talked swimming and cricket with the subalterns, until, catching the monitory eye of Dr. Bruno and observing that Trelawny was getting obstreperous, he rose to go. At once his vigilant Tita signalled for the boat, into the stern-sheets of which, with much laughter and many festive farewells, the guests eventually were bundled down the bastion-side.

The lights of the mess and the glow of the Officers' cigars, reflected dancingly in the black water, gradually diminished astern; and in the pervading stillness the moon in a spangled sky diffused enchantment on the landlocked bay, lazy as a lagoon. But as they drew out a little, a breeze came down the corries of the surrounding hills, crinkling the surface of the black-burnished water, and Trelawny stepped a small mast forward while Tita took the tiller; for though the howling of Byron's dogs on board was distinctly audible, the *Hercules* lay some distance from shore. Except the ever watchful Tita, Byron's companions by now were half asleep. A cloud obscured the moon for a moment, and there fell a chilly spot or two of rain. The boat seemed to be rushing with the run of the water into the arms of night.

Byron shivered a little, and drew his boat-cloak closer.

*   *   *   *   *

The Napiers of Merchiston were a brilliant but unaccountable family of Lothian lairds. In the sixteenth century, John Napier spent his days in petty litigation with his kinsfolk and neighbours and yet had time to invent logarithms, the first hydraulic pump, and the earliest calculating machine: while Sir Archibald was not only a Master of the Mint, but an authority on matters mining and ecclesiastical. In the seventeenth century the first and second Lords Napier were soldiers and agriculturists, who had both suffered for their association with Montrose. And in 1788 Colonel George, an early pupil of David Hume, was Officer-Superintendent at Woolwich and an expert on explosives. Of the two Charles Napiers who were to lend lustre to the name in the earlier nineteenth century, one was in 1823 a half-pay Captain R.N., who had served with distinction in America and the Mediterranean but was now in Paris promoting a scheme for iron steamers on the Seine, preparatory to hoisting his flag as a Portuguese Admiral, and afterwards his broad pennant as a victorious British Commodore fighting for the Porte at Acre and Beyrout against Mohammed Ali. The other, his cousin, George Napier's son Colonel Charles James, was

'King Tom's' Resident in Cephalonia, where he had
originally been sent in 1813 as an Inspecting Officer. As a
young C.O. of the 50th Foot (now the Royal West Kent
Regiment) he had been wounded and taken prisoner when
Moore fell at Corunna; since when he had served with
brilliance both regimentally and on the Staff in the Penin-
sular and American wars. The man who was destined to
be the conqueror of Scinde was now forty-one and a C.B.
A fine soldier with great force of character and decision
and a mordant sense of humour, he was apt to maintain
his own opinions against his superiors to the point of
insubordination: it was said of him that he either exceeded
his instructions or ignored them. He had already made
extended tours in Albania and on the Greek mainland,
examining the Graeco-Turkish question on the spot; and
had returned from these a convinced Philhellene, per-
suaded that the establishment of Greek independence was
not only bare justice to the Greeks, for whom he conceived
a sympathetic admiration, but essential for the maintenance of British maritime superiority in the eastern
Mediterranean. Though short-sighted, and lame in one
of his legs, Napier was essentially a man of action and a
fighter; and he had devoted many laborious months—with
Pitt-Kennedy, whom he made his First Commissioner
of Works—to matters of internal administration on the
Island, such as coastal lighting and wharfage, sanitation
and highways. "I would rather", he was to write afterwards, "have finished the roads of Cephalonia than have
fought Austerlitz or Waterloo." He told Trelawny that

the real requirements for the success of Byron's plans in Greece were "two European regiments, money in hand to pay them—and a portable gallows". Such was the Officer whom King Tom and a capricious Fate had entrusted with the enforcement of 'the strictest British neutrality' in Cephalonia. He was of all men the most likely to have distrusted Byron's theatricality and indefinite romanticism, his motley entourage, and his vague aspirations to be the hero of Greek deliverance. Yet Byron and he took to each other from the first. Napier realized the value to the Greek cause of Byron's name and fame throughout Europe and position in the English aristocracy: while Byron felt inspired by Napier's military resourcefulness and energy and his political and administrative sagacity, contact with which went far to dissipate his own increasing nervousness and self-distrust. He saw in the Colonel the type of man-of-action that he longed to be: he felt that Charles Napier could 'get things done', and he was not to be disappointed. It was the resolution with which the future victor of Meanee imbued him that sent him to Missolonghi the succeeding spring and paved the way for Navarino and the Treaty of London.

II

HEADQUARTERS AT METAXATA

Well, it seems that I am to be Commander-in-Chief, and
the post is by no means a sinecure, for we are not what Major
Sturgeon calls 'a set of the most amicable Officers!'

BYRON'S DIARY

Screen'd from espial by the jutting cape
That rears on high its rude fantastic shape,
Then rose his band to duty—not from sleep—
Equipp'd for deeds alike on land or deep;
While lean'd their leader o'er the fretting flood
And calmly talk'd—and yet he talked of blood.

THE military atmosphere in which Byron found himself at
Argostoli centred his vaguely heroic plans and ambitions
round a definite and practical nucleus of aggressive action.
This thing must come to fighting. The persistent and
sentimental attraction which Greece had held for him
since his earlier visits had since February been gradually
hardening to this conclusion. In March Captain Edward
Blaquière, a retired Officer and the travelling commissioner
of the Greek Committee of Philhellenes in London, had
called on him in Genoa with Andreas Luriottis, a delegate
of the Greek Revolutionary Council, and had fully explained to him the tactical and strategical position as it
then existed between the Turkish garrisons and the in-

surgents. The result of this conference had been Byron's "offer of service with the Greeks", which the Committee accepted, at the same time co-opting him as a member. In May Hobhouse had written suggesting the formation of a Brigade; a plan which Byron modified very sensibly by proposing instead the recruitment of a few experienced Officers (preferably of Artillery and Engineers) and the provision of large consignments of suitable munitions. Instead of by the enrolment of a rabble of scallywags from anywhere just 'game for a scrap', the rank and file could be furnished later and more usefully from among the best fighting material available in the country itself. As to the Officers who might volunteer, he begged they might be assured "that they are not going to rough it on beefsteak and a bottle of port, and that Greece was never plentifully stocked for a mess". Then had followed arrangements for finance with the English bank in Genoa and for stores with Henry Dunn, the 'Whiteley' of Leghorn, and finally the chartering of the *Hercules*, a 120-ton English collier brig. One important detail Byron's characteristic vanity forbade him to overlook—the provision of proper uniforms for himself and his Staff. He sat to a Genoese artist for his portrait, arrayed in a portentous brass helmet (executed to his order by Aspe the goldsmith) with metal chin-strap, a formidable plume, and the Byron arms engraved above the peak. Trelawny was to wear such another, and Gamba a Uhlan's shako of green and black leather, fronted with the emblem of Athené. The tunics were to be of gold-laced scarlet. Trelawny, however, jeered at all such warlike millinery, which Byron therefore peevishly discarded, contenting himself with his green cavalry jacket and gilt-banded forage-cap and the spare uniform of an Officer in the 8th which he borrowed later from Colonel Duffie at Argostoli. Constantine Mavrocordato, whose brother was the provisional Premier of Western Greece, wrote to him at Genoa suggesting Missolonghi, at the north-western end of the Gulf of Corinth, as a base of operations, where Byron and his Brigade could get into touch with Botzaris and the Souliote tribesmen, and commence an offensive with them against the Turks in Epirus. This letter and advice was followed, however, by a dispatch from Blaquière counselling delay on the ground that the situation on the western mainland was as yet too involved and incoherent to be favourable for immediate action.

But Byron was sick of kicking his heels in Genoa. He had spoken of himself and thought of himself as a man of action—a man of action who had been driven by circumstance to use that trivial instrument the pen. Here at last was a chance to prove it. And so in mid-July the brig *Hercules* was towed past the *Fanale* and out to sea by the boats of an American corvette.

*   *   *   *   *

Edward Blaquière was right, however. Neither at Byron's end nor at the proposed front were matters ripe for action with any prospect of even the most moderate success. Disunion, as Thucydides showed in a famous passage in his Third Book, was the cause of the wars that wrecked Hellenic civilization; and disunion was still the obstacle to its reassertion. The Greek patriots, both in the field and in the council-chamber, were, like their followers, at hopeless loggerheads, divided by intrigues and jealousies into Eastern and Western sections; money was not available in sufficient quantity and munitions were to seek. Therefore, refusing Napier's offer of a room in the Residency at Argostoli (in apprehension, perhaps, of what 'King Tom' might do if he got to hear of such an indiscretion), Byron hired a house at Metaxata, a village four miles down the coast at the extreme south-westerly point of the island; and, having paid off the *Hercules*, settled down there in September with his Staff to await events and develop his plan of action in masterly inactivity. "I like this place", said Byron, with reference to Metaxata; "I don't know why—but I dislike to move. There aren't, to be sure, many allurements here; neither from the commodiousness of the house nor the bleak view of the Black Mountain. There is no learned society nor the presence of beautiful women; and yet, for all that, I would wish to remain; as I have found myself more comfortable and my time passes more cheerfully than it has for a long time done." But he got on with the beginnings of his Brigade, for he enlisted some forty of the most likely among the Souliote refugees under their chiefs Djavella and Draco, and abandoning an idea to constitute them his personal bodyguard at Headquarters, shipped them over to Missolonghi in advance with two months' pay and the arms and ammunition which the British had impounded from them on their arrival. (He had a sentimental obsession for the untrustworthy and undisciplinable Souliotes; they looked so bravely romantic; their fustanella kilts and tasselled shoe-toes were so picturesque;

> On Souli's rock and Parga's shore
>   Exists the remnant of a line
> Such as the Doric mothers bore
>   And there perhaps some seed is sown
> The Heracleidan blood might own.

In September Trelawny left Metaxata to join Hamilton Browne 'on Intelligence' in the Morea—he was never to see Byron again, alive.

At Headquarters time passed busily and pleasantly enough: Byron swam and rode and boated, and drank gin-and-water with the subalterns of the 8th when they rode over from Argostoli; while conducting a ceaseless corres-pondence about men and money with the London Com-mittee, the bankers at home and in the Mediterranean, and the Greek leaders, for ever quarrelling among them-selves. As to finance, funds were never satisfactory, and Byron was pledging his private resources up to the hilt. He had written to 'Doug.' Kinnaird—an old friend of Hob-house's and his in London, who varied his business as head of Ransome's Bank by playwriting and membership of the Greek Committee—instructing him "to get together all the means and credit of mine we can to face the war establishment; for it is 'in for a penny in for a pound', and I must do all that I can for the ancients. I have now advanced them four thousand pounds."

Napier and Pitt-Kennedy and other Officers from Argostoli and Ithaca were constantly in and out; and 'King Tom' sent his Government Secretary down from Corfu to see what was going on. This official, unexpectedly enough, proved to be Lord Sidney Osborne, a son, by a second marriage, of the Duke of Leeds whose first wife had run away with 'Mad Jack Byron' the Poet's disreputable father, then an ex-guardsman, by whom she became the mother of Augusta Leigh. Notwithstanding this embarrassing connection, Byron and Osborne foregathered quite amicably, and the latter's reports to Corfu were not of such a nature as in any way to prejudice Byron's plans. October brought George Finlay, the future historian of Greece but then an undergraduate at Göttingen with such a startling personal resemblance to Shelley that it disconcerted Byron, who promptly sent him off 'on Intelligence' to Athens; for he knew that Finlay was fond of the Greeks and was fluent in their language. (Finlay ultimately bought a property in Attica where he lived the rest of his life.) So the long autumn wore on, and in November arrived Dr. Julius Millengen, with the earliest of the Officer recruits. These were three German Officers, all gunners—Major Baron von Quass and Lieutenants Kindermann and Fels—who were at once dispatched to make a beginning with the artillery unit at Missolonghi, where Millengen, a foppish and effeminate young doctor from Edinburgh who had been sent out by the London Committee in charge of medical stores collected by the Society of Friends, rejoined them in December.

At the end of November Byron's Staff was reinforced by two more 'Officers of experience', sent out respectively by the German and English Philhellene Committees. The first was a Colonel Delaunay, a German *Oberst*, notwithstanding his French name; and the second was Lieutenant-Colonel the Hon. Leicester Fitzgerald Stanhope, C.B., later fifth Earl of Harrington, who, during what was left of Byron's lifetime, was to be his thorn-in-the-flesh, and after his death was to bring home the barrel containing the box that held his body. An Officer then of twenty-four years' service—which included the attack on Buenos Aires and a period as D.Q.M.G. in India during the Mahratta War—he was also, unfortunately, a doctrinaire politician and educationist and a fanatical Benthamite, who never ceased the asseveration in and out of season of his republican ideas and of his determination to imbue the Greek patriots with Liberal principles by the establishment among them of a 'Free Press'; which, though ninety per cent of the inhabitants of Greece were hopelessly illiterate, he seemed to think would be a more effective instrument towards national liberty then mere force of arms. Napier and he were as oil and water: the sole subject on which they registered an agreement was the necessity of somehow 'getting on'. And as autumn slid into winter, it became increasingly clear that the continued internal dissensions among the Greek Commanders and political leaders were developing into something very like civil war, and at any rate precluding proper concerted action in an offensive against the Turks. Upon the advice, *mirabile dictu*, of both of these mutually antagonistic Officers, Byron in early December wrote an open letter to the Greek 'Government', pointing out that, unless such internecine discord was discontinued, the flotation of the projected Loan to finance the movement would be irredeemably prejudiced and any forward movement rendered impossible. Stanhope was then sent to present this ultimatum in person to Mavrocordato at Missolonghi, where he was also authorized to establish the artillery unit and organize a base hospital—and, if it pleased him, an educational establishment, a Free Press, and such other blessings of a Benthamite civilization as he might think fit; provided only he could get things going. Within a short time of his arrival he wrote back—and the dispatch arrived with others in a similar tenor from Mavrocordato himself and the 'Greek Senate' at Salamis —urging Byron with vehemence to proceed at once to Missolonghi for instant action. It was obvious to all at Metaxata that the time had come; and Byron moved accordingly. At once he shifted his staff to Argostoli, and chartered a couple of Cephalonian ships to convey the party to the mainland under the neutrality of the Ionian flag. The larger of these, called in the naval parlance of the day a 'Bombard', was a roomy flat-bottomed sailing-barge which would take the servants, the 'chargers'—six horses bought by Byron long ago in the Romagna—and the bulkier baggage: and the smaller, a long fast-sailing open-decked felucca with lateen rig, locally and romantically termed a 'Mystico', was selected by Byron to carry himself, the money, and his Officers. On Boxing Day 1823 the wind was contrary when they embarked, and both ships put back into Argostoli, when the travellers returned to shore and put up at the house of Mr. Hancock, the local English banker, to wait wearily for a change in the weather. This came on the 28th, but found the party scattered. Count Gamba, who as Chief-of-Staff looked after finances and carried all the cash, was having a farewell tea with Dr. Kennedy, the P.M.O. of the Argostoli garrison. On being summoned he left at once, and with all the money boarded, not the Mystico as arranged, but the Bombard. Fletcher, Byron's English valet, was run to earth after a hue-and-cry, having a final drink with the servants at the Officers' Mess. Legà Zambelli, my Lord's Italian steward, with the negro groom and Lucas Chalandritsanos, a refugee boy whom Byron had made his page, had all to be rounded up with difficulty. Byron himself was reading a novel of Scott's in Hancock's study; but eventually the whole party—even Byron's bull-dog *Moretto* and his New-foundland *Lion*, the successor of *Boatswain* of Newstead days and a present to him from Lieutenant le Mesurier, an English Naval Officer on the station—were safely put aboard their respective craft, which at once headed south-ward with a following wind for Zante, where stores and specie were awaiting them. From Zante on the evening of the 29th they hoisted sail at last for the mainland; and the crews, who realized by now the nature of the enterprise and the importance of their passengers, broke into patriotic songs of Hellas as they hauled at the halyards. With his hand on a stanchion Byron watched them in the highest fettle, cheerful and full of confidence. His torturing self-distrust when faced with practical responsibilities, which, he was conscious, had condoned the long delay in Cephalonia, was for the moment thrust aside. A man of action, his elation soared. He was childishly pleased because the Mystico was the faster ship; and, as night fell, ordered signals to be fired by a preconcerted code of pistol-flashes to the slower Bombard, labouring far astern in the trough of the swell: "To-morrow we meet at Missolonghi—to-morrow!"

III

THE 'BRIGADE' AT MISSOLONGHI

With me there is, as Napoleon said, but one step between
the sublime and the ridiculous. Well, *if* I do (and this *if* is
a grand *peut-être* in my future history) outlive the campaign,
I shall write two poems on the subject—one an Epic and the
other a Burlesque.

> Now at length we're off to Turkey
> Lord knows when we shall come back!
> Breezes foul and tempests murky
> May unship us in a crack.

OLYMPUS is a far cry from Missolonghi, but such of the
gods as disapproved of Byron's *Iliad* clearly determined to
make it disagreeable for him from the first. To begin with,
though their ship was the slower, Gamba and the Bombard
party arrived at Missolonghi before Byron—but without
the Bombard. For, after losing touch with the Mystico
during the night, that luckless craft was captured next
morning by a Turkish frigate, which, after Gamba had
thrown overboard his confidential papers, she had to follow
to the port of Patras (beyond Missolonghi and on the
opposite side of the Gulf) for official examination by the
enemy authorities. But here such deities as were favourable
to Greece and Byron interposed; and the Cretan captain of
the frigate, having discovered that the Bombard's skipper

was the very man who had saved him from shipwreck some years before, fell on his neck with tears; and, although he was told the whole truth, promised to see them through. That evening he gave dinner in his cabin to the skipper and Gamba, who swallowed the meal with relief while their host undertook to make his superiors swallow with equal ease his guests' story of the Bombard being merely an Ionian vessel proceeding to Kalamos in the service of an English milord. Next day he was as good as his word with the local Pasha, who, after deliberating for three days (which Gamba spent shooting woodcock), released all the suspects and sent them on January 4 with the horses and all the cargo intact across to Missolonghi.

The Mystico, meanwhile, had a similarly disconcerting experience. For when entering the Gulf on the night of the 29th she was hailed by a Turkish ship, which, as the sun rose, she only managed to elude by creeping cautiously among the shallows of the Aetolian coast to Dragomestri, many miles north of her objective. From here Byron sent Lucas Chalandritsanos as a runner to Mavrocordato at Missolonghi, asking for an escort for a march thither by land. But on January the 3rd a message came back informing Byron that this was impracticable, and that a convoy ship was being sent round Cape Scropha. The Greek brig *Leonidas* shortly afterwards appeared, and with this protection the Mystico got under weigh again. But the quarrelling on Olympus, apparently, still continued; and the anti-Byron gods determined that he should perpetuate the reputation of his grandfather the Admiral, 'Foul-weather Jack', who never put to sea without a gale. Squalls blew all day on the 4th: twice did the Mystico run ashore, to be refloated only with blood and tears; and it was not until darkness fell that she could at last anchor off Missolonghi, at the west entrance to the lagoon.

The following morning Byron prepared to land and assume command. To make the occasion as impressive as possible he discarded the old cavalry jacket and, 'King Tom' or no 'King Tom', put on the uniform which had been lent to him by Colonel Duffie. And so, rowed ashore in a *monoxylon* with the new blue-and-white ensign of Independent Greece fluttering bravely from its jackstaff, the long looked-for *Strategos Veeron* made his second landing in Hellas—arrayed this time as an Officer of His Britannic Majesty's 8th Foot—and was greeted with gunfire, *feux de joie* of musketry, and a tumult of welcoming cheers from the assembled patriots. Count Gamba, who had never thought to see his Chief again, burst into tears; Prince Mavrocordato, a plump Pickwickian figure, beamed rapturously through his spectacles; but Byron, after receiving the reports of Stanhope and the rest, proceeded at once to his Headquarters in 'the House of Capsali', overlooking the lagoon, to shed his tight uniform and have a bath. He had not rested or taken off his clothes (except for the uniform) since leaving Argostoli a week before.

* * * * *

Fletcher and Legà Zambelli at once got busy shelving

Byron's books and arranging trophies of arms on the walls
of his sitting-room; while Byron, now formally appointed
Archistrategos, sat on a divan, presiding over a council-of-
war of all the chiefs and primates of Western Greece who
had been assembled by Mavrocordato to await his arrival.
In view of the reports that the Turks were likely in the
early spring to launch an offensive against Missolonghi
from their fortresses at Patras and Lepanto on either side
the entrance to the Gulf of Corinth, it was decided, after
protracted deliberations and on confidential reports from
'Intelligence' that its garrison were quite willing to be
bought, to forestall such action by an attack on the latter
fortress: the assaulting columns to be conveyed there in the
five Greek brigs then at Missolonghi, whose crews, if an
advance of pay were guaranteed, affirmed that they would
undertake the duty. The constitution and efficiency of the
attacking force at once became a matter of urgent importance. First, as to artillery. The London Committee
had promised to send out an artillery expert with a staff of
artificers, who might be expected to arrive at any moment.
The Officers available were Major von Quass and his pair
of German subalterns, with a few young Philhellene volunteers who had drifted down to Missolonghi at odd times.
The men were enrolled from among the most likely of the
assembled polyglot volunteers and native patriots, and on
January the 20th this bobbery pack of gunners was installed in the Seraglio, a ramshackle building presenting to
the naked eye but little of the seductiveness connoted by
its name. As to infantry, five hundred of the Souliote

refugees under Djavella and his rival Chief Draco, a picturesque but undisciplined rabble with their fustanella kilts and motley weapons, were formed into a battalion, which began at once tumultuously to drill—in the rare intervals between the Officers' jealous altercations and the violent personal vendettas of the 'other ranks'—in the courtyard of the House of Capsali just under Byron's windows.

January the 18th brought bad news: the Turkish fleet was out from Patras and had established a blockade of the Gulf, while the five patriot brigs had fled before them— thus gravely compromising the transport plan for the attack on Lepanto. Byron was for an immediate 'cutting-out' expedition in boats, under his personal command, to break the blockade; and from this plan he was with difficulty dissuaded. It was decided instead to wait and to make some fresh arrangement for sea-transport. The 22nd was Byron's thirty-sixth birthday, and, reversing the usual custom, he presented his Staff with some verses—the last he was to finish—dated accordingly and headed "On this Day I complete my Thirty-sixth Year".

'Tis time this heart should be unmoved,
　Since others it has ceased to move:
Yet, though I cannot be beloved,
　Still let me love!

My days are in the yellow leaf;
　The flowers and fruits of love are gone:
The worm, the canker, and the grief
　Are mine alone.

The fire that on my bosom preys
  Is lone as some volcanic isle;
No torch is kindled at its blaze—
  A funeral pile.

The hope, the fear, the jealous care,
  The exalted portion of the pain
And power of love, I cannot share,
  But wear the chain.

But 'tis not thus—and 'tis not here—
  Such thoughts should shake my soul, nor now,
Where glory decks the hero's bier,
  Or binds his brow.

(The remaining verses appear at the beginning and the end of this chapter. They are poignantly prophetic, and express the poet's determination to devote himself to the cause of Greek liberty, with what Moore called the "consciousness of a near grave glimmering sadly through the whole". When reading them to his Staff Byron remarked that he thought they were "better than what I usually write".)

Stanhope had installed a printing-press at Headquarters and was busy trying to issue numbers of a paper, *The Greek Chronicle*, to inculcate Benthamite principles among the illiterate patriots. Byron laughed at him and said that the poet was likely to have his artillery brigade ready before the soldier had fixed his printing-press: and while he contributed £50 towards Press expenses, made it clear that he regarded this journalistic propaganda as of less importance than the arrival of the ordnance experts; for that, at any rate, meant progress with the plan for attacking

Lepanto, where, as *Don Juan* the popinjay turned Paladin, the man of ease transformed into the man of action, he purposed to repeat the triumph of Don John of Austria against the Paynim.

Meanwhile, the Foreign Office in London, urged, as is not unlikely, by 'King Tom's' reports or by representations from the Porte, sent Captain Yorke, R.N., of H.M.S. *Alacrity*, to protest against infractions of Ionian neutrality by the Greek Provisional Government. Byron and Stanhope had a violent quarrel as to the appropriate action to be taken on this, in the midst of which the 'artillery experts' arrived. The London Committee had been advised in this matter by Colonel Thomas Gordon, not a gunner, but an Officer of the Scots Greys who had served in the Russian Army with Prince Ypsilanti and as a volunteer in the latter's force of cosmopolitan Philhellenes which had been disastrously routed by the Turks at Tripolizza three years before. (He subsequently commanded the expedition for the relief of Athens in 1827 and was made a Major-General in the Greek Army.) His advice was that they should send out as soon as possible to Missolonghi a 'Firemaster' or master-gunner, skilled in the making of all kinds of projectiles, explosives, and arms, with a few artificers in charge of the necessary apparatus and materials. The Firemaster would be able to recondition the large amount of spoiled powder in the possession of the Greeks, and to construct a battery of the famous Congreve incendiary rockets, the *flammenwerfer* of the period—invented by Sir William Congreve, Comptroller of Woolwich

Laboratory—which had been the terror of the French at Leipzig in 1813. With his stores and assistants this Crichton among artillerists arrived on February the 7th in the person of William Parry, who had been a Firemaster in the Royal Navy and afterwards a clerk in Woolwich Arsenal. He was a rough burly fellow, shrewd though unintelligent, with the gruff sentimentality of the lower deck; conceited, self-opinionated, and pot-valiant—for he drank like a fish. His plausible plain-spokenness commended him to Byron, satiated with Stanhope's Benthamite vapourings and Gamba's muddling diffidence: and for his part Parry developed a doglike devotion to his Chief that rivalled Tita Falchieri's, together with a surly detestation for most of the other members of the Staff. From the outset he styled himself 'Major Parry of Lord Byron's Brigade, Commanding Officer of Artillery and Engineers in the Service of the Greeks'; and Byron chaffed him good-naturedly and made him his Chief Accountant, as well as assistant artillery Commandant under Stanhope. Parry and he were much together; and Byron, tired to death and harassed into a state of nervous agitation by his growing consciousness of his own failure as a man of action, the bickerings of his Officers, and the indiscipline of his men, began to solace himself with his Firemaster's favourite anodyne for worries—Brandy. This helped to soften the blow of his discovery that Parry had not the slightest idea of how to make Congreve rockets, that his apparatus required coal—of which there was none—and that Baron von Quass had sent in his resignation sooner than serve under the new artillerist. Byron comforted himself with yet another brandy and the news that the Lepanto garrison was more pressingly anxious than ever to surrender—for a consideration; with a shrug, he sent to the Bank at Zante for more money, and signed a requisition for some old guns which he was told were lying about somewhere in Corinth.

But matters were moving at last; and he issued orders that the Souliote Infantry under Gamba should prepare to proceed to Lepanto as advance-guard on February the 14th. The anti-Byron deities, however, took a hand once more; for when the Souliotes got their orders they promptly struck for increased pay and the immediate promotion to commissioned rank of nearly half their number. The thing was becoming tragically grotesque! In passionate anger Byron paraded the battalion and disbanded it; reconstituting from the remnants who were willing loyally to submit to discipline a smaller corps under his own immediate command. The strain and worry were taxing him too severely, and the same evening he had an alarming warning, an earnest of worse to follow, an epileptic fit—treated by the devoted Firemaster and Lieutenant Hesketh, Stanhope's *Aide*, with copious doses of brandy. He was put to bed immediately; but within half an hour two drunken German artillerymen, who had witnessed the trouble with the infantry in the morning, forced their way into his bedroom with an alarm that the Souliotes had mutinied and were marching on the Seraglio to seize the stores and ammunition. Stanhope at once paraded his gunners to defend the armoury, and all the sentries were doubled: but the alarm died down. Next morning Byron was bled, and nearly died from misapplication of the leeches by the nervous fumbling of Millengen and Bruno. Exhausted with pain and weak as a kitten, he could only listen listlessly to the next thrilling report: a Turkish brig had stranded on the coast not far away, and Parry was off at once with some gunners to capture its armament and stores. He waved his acquiescence with a feeble hand. Nothing much mattered now. He knew now that he could never be and had never been a man of action. It was obvious that he could not, and that the Souliotes would not, go to Lepanto. The set-piece had collapsed. Good-bye to all *Don Juan's* hopes of eclipsing Don John.

IV

FINALE

He who springs up a Hercules at once
Nurs'd in effeminate arts from youth to manhood,
And rushes from the banquet to the battle
As though it were a bed of love, deserves
. . . a Greek tomb his monument . . .

ON February the 18th, spent and faint from the effects of
his fit, Byron lay and received reports of the failure of the
attack on the brig. Gamba and Parry between them had
muddled all the arrangements, and the Turks managed to
take off their stores and ammunition and to blow up the
ship. But, as if this was not enough, next day Byron's
Olympian enemies redoubled their efforts among the
Souliotes. One of these ruffians, by name Toti, approached
the Seraglio with a small boy, a nephew of one of the
Souliote chiefs, to show the child the guns. The gunner
sentry at the gate, according to orders, forbade his entrance;
whereon the Souliote lost his temper and tried to push his
way in. The sentry called for the sergeant of the guard, a
Hungarian, who used force to expel the Souliote. A struggle
ensued and in response to the sergeant's calls for the guard
to turn out, Lieutenant Sass (a Swede), the Officer of the
guard, ran out and struck the Souliote with the flat of his

sabre. The Souliote saw red. He drew sword and pistol, and, attacking the Officer, severed his left arm and shot him through the head. The guard confined the murderer at once, and the news ran like wildfire through Missolonghi. The whole body of Souliotes mobbed the arsenal, trained the guns outside it against the gateway, and threatened to set fire to it unless Toti were set free. Byron convened an immediate meeting of Officers in his room, at which it was decided that all the Souliotes should at once be ordered to leave the place, and that unless this order was complied with, Byron himself would do so with all the foreign Officers and volunteers.

To promulgate this decision, Byron, weak as he still was, put on his most impressive uniform (which must have been that of the 8th Foot, for his only other was the cavalry jacket), and convened what Napier would have called a *jirgeh* of these truculent tribesmen. The Souliote chiefs attended in full costume, while the tribesmen, muttering and gesticulating, crowded the entrances. Byron delivered his ultimatum, which was deceptively accepted; and the chiefs, promising that 'justice should be done', put on their shoes and withdrew. But they and their followers did not leave the town until the local civic authorities had paid them 3000 dollars 'as a loan', advanced, of course, out of the pocket of the *Archistrategos*. Six out of the eight artillery artificers followed their example, claiming to be sent back home because the murder of Sass had shown that the clause in their contract with the London Committee of 'employment only in a place of safety' could no longer be

fulfilled. Parry was thus left with two artificers only.
Under these repeated blows Byron's head was bloody but
unbowed. Stanhope and Gamba had urged him to leave,
but by now he had formed the determination not to run
away; and the tragic tale of disaster was continued. On
February the 21st there was an earthquake and a flood—
but Stanhope left on confidential business for Athens.
Next day there was a slight temporary recurrence of
Byron's epilepsy, but some further foreign recruits arrived
for the artillery; and Finlay rode in from Athens with dis-
patches from Trelawny and the Eastern Greek leaders,
who, dissenting from Byron's plans, had begun to intrigue
against him. The month of March saw some improvement
in Byron's health and he managed to hobble about supervising the reorganization of the artillery and the improvement of the defences.

But the virus of indiscipline attacked even the foreign
Officers of the artillery, one of whom robbed and mal-
treated a Greek and had to be reduced to the ranks. The
Brigade was paraded and the ceremonial of official degrada-
tion duly carried out. Resentment at this sentence and the
sudden emergence of many petty jealousies resulted in a
succession of challenges and duels. In Colonel Stanhope's
absence Major Parry was in command, and on his suggestion Byron, as *Archistrategos*, put all the artillery Officers
under arrest. Under these cumulative anxieties Byron
became increasingly irritable and hypochondriacal. The
weather broke, and for the next month the spring sirocco
blew with tempestuous fury. All progress appeared to be at

a standstill. Trelawny wrote from Athens announcing that a conference between the leaders of the eastern and western wings of the Greek Emancipationists would be held at Salona in Attica on March the 28th, at which it was hoped that their mutual variances and internecine quarrels would be finally buried and some concerted movement against the Turks decided on. Tired of inaction in the mud and misery at Missolonghi, Byron determined to attend with Mavrocordato and to lend such influence as he still possessed to this belated policy of co-operation. But a fresh trouble intervened. Since their expulsion from Missolonghi in February the mutinous Souliotes had been roving about the districts north and west of the lagoons looting and committing excesses. They ultimately joined forces with one Karäiskaki, a local independent chief whose nephew, on April the 1st, was wounded in a scrimmage with some Missolonghiote boatmen. At once Karäiskaki demanded redress and monetary compensation from Byron and sent a large force of his followers against the town to press his demands. He further arranged with Djavella and his section of the Souliotes to march on Missolonghi from the north-west, and entered into a traitorous arrangement with the Turkish Admiral at Patras to blockade the place from the sea; hoping by these means to overthrow Byron and Mavrocordato and obtain their funds and munitions. Up to a point the scheme was successful: Djavella seized the fort at Vasiladi which commanded the entrance to the lagoon, and some Turkish war-vessels appeared in the roadstead outside. Ill and dejected as he was, Byron spurred

himself into activity,—one last attempt to prove he was a
man of action. He put the town into a state of defence,
and, partly to test the strength of the treacherous attackers,
partly to reassure the panic-stricken inhabitants, ordered a
reconnaissance on April the 6th. The column marched
through the town and three miles out into the hinterland
beyond. The advance-guard was furnished by a company
of the loyal Souliote infantry, behind which, on one of his
Romagna horses, rode the *Archistrategos* in his cavalry jacket
and gold and blue forage cap, attended by Lambro, his
favourite Souliote orderly and followed by his personal
Staff, Gamba, Bruno, and the rest, with Tita Falciere in a
chasseur's uniform of blue and silver, young Lucas Chalandritsanos in a scarlet livery, and the negro groom. A second
company of the Souliotes brought up the rear. Not a shot
was fired, for no enemy were discoverable in the area
covered. Something must have miscarried with Karäiskaki's
plans, for next day Djavella evacuated the fort and the
Turkish ships were seen hull-down on the horizon. But it
was quite obvious that in the circumstances Byron could
not risk the journey to Salona for the conference. On the
9th Byron rode out again three miles into the country with
Gamba and an orderly, having arranged to return by boat.
The weather was oppressively thundery, and a violent rain-
storm broke suddenly before they reached the boat. Gamba
advised riding back to avoid the risk of a chill while sitting
soaked with rain and perspiration on the thwarts. But
Byron refused: "I should make a pretty soldier", he protested, "if I were to care for such a trifle." That night he

had a shivering fit, with pains in the back and limbs. But on the 10th he was in the saddle again, going round the defences with Gamba and his Staff;—it was afterwards remembered that he had then checked the negro groom for not having changed the saddle, which was still damp from the previous day's downpour. In the evening he complained of fever and shivering and called in Bruno. His dejection had sapped all power of resistance, for he no longer doubted that he would be of better service to the cause dead than alive. Major Parry was at last alarmed and proposed crossing next day to Zante where the climate and accommodation were better and English doctors were available. But on the 11th and for days thereafter the sirocco blew its worst and a move was impossible. A slight improvement on the 15th was followed by a serious relapse, with some delirium. Bruno and Millengen, nervous and agitated with unprofessional emotion, were scarcely reassuring medical attendants; the servants crowded round the sick-room, frightened and whispering and too tearfully solicitous; while Parry hovered near with his sovran remedy of the brandy-bottle.

Byron was bled and drenched and bled again, convulsed with pain and gasping incoherently in Italian and English. The delirium increased in violence, and at intervals was succeeded by even more terrifying periods of coma.

Outside, the thunder muttered and rumbled and the sirocco lashed the house with sheets of driving rain. Byron's Olympian enemies were working with Homeric thoroughness, marshalling even the elements as instru-

ments of their displeasure. And on Monday, April the
19th, Easter Monday, they had their way. All day he had
been comatose, and in the evening at a quarter-past six he
opened his eyes for an instant—and closed them finally.
Fletcher, his faithful English valet, moved for a moment
out of the well-trained impassivity which for ten years had
stood the strain of Byronic service, turned to the doctors
and cried piteously, "My God! I fear his Lordship is
gone!"

Fletcher was right. He would have to seek another situation. His Lordship's despairing effort to live as a man of
action had failed. Death was the one thing he had left to
offer. *Childe Harold's* pilgrimage was over; the Brigade had
lost its Commander and Greece her most chivalrous and
disinterested champion.

*　　*　　*　　*　　*

The minute guns which boomed from Parry's battery at
dawn were answered by joyful salvos from the Turkish
artillery down the Gulf at Patras and Lepanto, for news
spreads quickly east of the Adriatic.

On the 21st, Captain Edward Blaquière arrived at Zante
in the *Florida* brig with a large consignment of money from
the Committee in London. The body was brought across
from Missolonghi on May the 30th for shipment home on
the *Florida*, and Colonel Stanhope came over to take charge,
having been peremptorily recalled to England by the Wa
Office at the urgent request of our Ambassador at Con-
stantinople, who had grown weary of the Porte's protests

against the continued infraction of British neutrality by a serving Officer. And on the 25th all that was left of Byron was carried away from the Ionian Islands, as he had arrived there nine months before, in an English brig.

* * * * *

On July the 5th Hobhouse, his oldest friend from Trinity days onward, boarded the *Florida* in London Docks to receive the barrelled coffin—at whose foot he found *Lion*, Byron's Newfoundland dog, lying on guard, as he had lain steadfastly all through the voyage.

* * * * *

> If thou regret'st thy youth, why live?
> The land of honourable death
> Is here:—up to the Field, and give
> Away thy breath!
>
> Seek out—less often sought than found—
> A Soldier's grave, for thee the best,
> Then look around, and choose thy ground,
> And take thy Rest.

LIST OF AUTHORITIES

AITKEN, G. A., *Life of Richard Steele*. 1882.

ARTHUR, Captain SIR GEORGE, *The Story of the Household Cavalry*. 1909.

CAINE, SIR H., *Life of Coleridge*. 1887.

COLVIN, SIR SIDNEY, *Landor*. 1888.

DOBSON, AUSTIN, *Richard Steele*. 1897.

DYKES, CAMPBELL, *Works of Coleridge*. 1894.

FORSTER, J., *Life and Works of Landor*. 1868.

GIBBON, EDWARD, Diary and Notes: *Decline and Fall of the Roman Empire*. 1853–67.

HOWITT, WILLIAM, *Homes and Haunts of the English Poets*. 1847.

LLOYD-VERNEY, COLONEL, *The Infantry Militia Battalions of the County of Southampton*. 1894.

LYNN LYNTON, Mrs., 'Landor': *Fraser's Magazine*. July 1870.

LOCKHART, JOHN GIBSON, *Life of Scott*. 1851.

MACAULAY, LORD, *Essay on Addison*. 1854.

MARSHALL, MAJOR J. R., 'Quartermaster Scott': *Blackwood's Magazine*. April 1930.

MAYNE, ETHEL COLBURN, *Byron*. 1912.

MORRISON, J. C., *Gibbon*. 1887.

NICHOLSON, HAROLD, *Byron, The Last Journey*. 1924.

PARRY, WILLIAM, *The Last Days of Lord Byron*. 1825.

STALKER, A., *The Intimate Life of Sir Walter Scott*. 1898.

TRAILL, H. D., *Coleridge*. 1884.

TRELAWNY, E. J., *Records of Shelley, Byron and the Author*. 1878.

INDEX

Blake, General, 166, 168, 169, 170
Blandford, 60, 61, 64, 68
Blandford of King's, 95
Blaquière, Captain Edward, 191, 193, 217
Blenheim, 38
Boatswain, 199
Bocage, Madame, 81
Bolton, the Duke of, 56, 57, 58, 62, 78
Border Minstrelsy, 139
Border Regiment, the [*see* 34th Foot]
Boroughbridge, 44
Boswell, James, 71
Bowyer, Dr., 94
Boyle, 39
Boyne, the Battle of the, 13, 18
Bramshill, 62
Brentford, 62
Brest, 160
Brighton, 152, 153, 156, 157
Bristol, 155
British Censor, the, 45
Broderick, General, 168, 173
Brown Adam, 139, 140, 146
Browne, Hamilton, 183, 185, 195
Bruno, Dr. Francesco, 183, 185, 186, 187, 210, 215, 216
Bruntsfield, 122, 126
Buccleuch, the Duke of, 112, 140
Bucks Militia, the, 71, 72
Buda, 18
Buenos Aires, 197
Buffs, the, 32, 62
Buonaparte, Joseph, 151, 170
Bürger, Gottfried, 112

Buriton, 51, 52, 54, 55, 58, 64, 69, 75, 76, 78, 79, 81, 82
Burrard, Sir Harry, 151
Busaco, the Battle of, 145
Bute, Lord, 71, 72, 73
Butler, Dr. S., 90, 93, 103
Butler, Samuel, 90
Byron, Lord, 179-218
Byron, the 5th Lord, 196

Cadiz, 32, 177
Calpe, Rock of, 150
Calshot Castle, 151
Camaret Bay, 16
Canning, George, 152, 172
Capsali, the House of, 203, 205
Captain, 138
Carisbrooke Castle, 16, 22
Carlisle, 117, 118
Carlos IV of Spain, 150
Carlyle, 154
Carrick Roads, the, 159
Caryll, John, 35
Castaños, 151
Cathcart, Lord, 142
Catt, Christopher, 36
Cavan, Lady, 41
Cephalonia, 181, 189, 190, 200
Cevallos, Don Pedro, 163, 176
Chalandritsanos, Lucas, 199, 202, 215
Charles I, 87
Charles II, 6, 7, 20, 39, 55
Charles VIII of Naples, 64
Charpentier, Charlotte [Lady Scott], 117, 127, 128, 138
Charterhouse, 3, 4, 10
Cherbourg, 160

INDEX

INDEX

INDEX

Laidlaw, Willie, 134
Lamb, Charles, 94
Lambro, 215
Lancelot du Lac, Sir, 114
Landen, 5
Landguard Fort, 30, 32, 33, 36, 37, 43
Landor, W. S., 26, 147-78
Landrecies, 88
Lara, 184
Laregovia, 162, 175
Lasswade, 112, 131, 132
Lausanne, 50, 52, 54, 81
Lay of the Last Minstrel, The, 131
Le Cateau, 88
Leeds, the Duke of, 196
Leghorn, 166, 192
Leigh, Augusta, 196
Leipzig, the Battle of, 208
Leith, 113, 122, 126, 134
Le Mesurier, R.N., Lieut., 199
Lenore, 122, 138
Leon, 168, 169, 170
Leonidas, 202
Lepanto, 204, 205, 207, 209, 210, 217
Lewis, Matthew ('Monk'), 112, 113
Lichfield, 90
Liddesdale, 138
Lieutenant, 138
Life Guards, the, 6, 7, 8, 9, 10, 13, 29, 35, 37
Lincoln's Inn, 144
Lion, 199, 218
Llanthony Abbey, 166
Lockhart, 124, 143
Lôk, 115

London Post, the, 10
London, Treaty of, 190
Londonderry, 12
Long, General, 111
Lorraine, 51
Lorraine, Duke of, 18
Lothians, the, 132
Louis XIV, 3, 7, 9, 14
Louis XVI, 53
Louis XVII, 87
Lovell, Robert, 154
Lucas, Lord, 30, 42
Lugo, 168, 173
Lumpkin, Tony, 59
Luriottis, Andreas, 191
Luxembourg, 51
Lying Lover, The, 25, 36
Lyons, 117

Macaulay, Lord, 11, 132
MacDougal of Mackerstoun, Sir George, 119
MacGregor, Colonel Murray, 135
Mackenzie of Auchindenny, 112
Mackenzie of Portmore, Colin, 116
Madrid, 149, 168, 169, 170, 172, 175, 176
Magdalen College, Oxford, 4, 52
Mahratta War, the, 197
Maidstone, 62
Maitland of Rankeillor, Major C., 113
Maitland, Sir Thomas, 182, 187, 189, 190, 194, 196, 203, 207
Mallets, the, 54
Malta, 182, 185

INDEX

Reynosa, 170, 171
Rhine, the, 115
Rich, Christopher, 29, 36
Robinson, Crabbe, 166
Rochefort, 177
Rogers, Captain Bill, 160
Roliça, the Battle of, 169
Rome, 81, 168
Romsey, 75
Ropley, 77
Rousseau, J. J., 53, 154
Roxburgh, 132
Royal Cinque Ports Light Dragoons, the, 113, 122
Royal Edinburgh Light Dragoons, the, 107-46
Royal Exchange Coffee House, the, 120
Royal Fusiliers, the, 55, 56
Royal Horse Guards, the, 6, 7
Royal Society, the, 39
Royal West Kent Regiment [see 50th Foot]
Rugby School, 153, 156, 162

Saint Abb's Head, 132
Saint Anthony's Point, 159
Saint Catherine's College, Cambridge, 18
Saint Germains, 14
Saint Jean-de-Luz, 160
Saint John's College, Cambridge, 90
Saint Mawes, 159
Saint Paul's, 16
Saint Petersburg, 177
Salamis, 198
Salona, 214, 215

Sandhurst, 146
Santerre, 87
Sass, Lieut., 211, 212
Schellenberg, 38
Scinde, 189
Scots Greys, the, 119, 207
Scots Guards, the, 20
Scott, John, 116, 119, 120
Scott, Robert, 138
Scott, Sir Walter, 107-46, 199
Scott, Sir Walter the Second, 145, 146
Scotus, Duns, 125
Scropha, Cape, 202
Sedley, Sir C., 22, 23
Seine, R., 188
Selkirk, 132
Selkirkshire Yeomanry, the, 133, 134
Selwyn, Mrs., 11
Sentry, Captain, 45
Seward, Miss, 143
Shakespeare, 102
Sheerness, 32
Sheffield, Lord, 81
Shelley, 196
Sheridan, R. B., 151
Shrewsbury School, 90
Sissinghurst, 62
Skene, Cornet James, 113, 121, 122, 124, 128, 130, 136, 138, 141, 144
Smith, Lieut., 77
Society of Friends, the, 196
Sophocles, 99
Somerset House, 8
Somerset Light Infantry, the [see 13th Foot]

INDEX

AUTHORS-AT-ARMS

THE END